Knowledge Management: The Death of Wisdom

Knowledge Management: The Death of Wisdom

Why Our Companies Have Lost It—and How They Can Get It Back

Third Edition

Arnold Kransdorff

businessexpert Press

First published in 2008 by
Business Expert Press, LLC
222 East 46th Street, New York, NY 10017
www.businessexpertpress.com

ISBN-13: 978-160649-542-1 (paperback)

ISBN-13: 978-160649-543-8 (e-book)

DOI 10.4128/ 9781606495421

Business Expert Press Strategic Management collection

Collection ISSN: 2150-9611 (print)
Collection ISSN: 2150-9646 (electronic)

Cover design by Jonathan Pennell
Interior design by Exeter Premedia Services Private Ltd., Chennai, India

First edition: 2008
Second edition: 2009
Third edition: 2012

10 9 8 7 6 5 4 3 2 1

Printed in the United States of America.

Abstract

Conceived less than 20 years ago, Knowledge Management (KM) is the business discipline about which managers perhaps know the least. Having spent pots of money investing in it, the benefits are still marginal. This is because practitioners are still feeling their way.

Now that the boom days are temporarily over, it is timely that KM can be more fully exploited, for it conceals an application that is indispensable for the foreseeable struggle ahead—and after, including an overlooked way out of the credit crash dilemma facing those dogmatic decision makers juggling the option between austerity and growth. It's not rocket science. It's a way of doing both, in this case by refocusing on the old-fashioned notion of productivity implied by this book's Chapter 2 heading: **Getting from A to B without going via Z**. Not the productivity that comes from cutbacks and austerity but the type that frontruns improved competitiveness, sales, and growth.

The journey to this solution is through the unacknowledged, iceberg-like, and delinquent edge to the enthusiastically pursued flexible labor market, a workplace development that is proving to be among the most corrosive of components to good decision making.

Whilst the ability to more easily hire 'n fire has allowed commerce and industry to more quickly refashion workforce numbers to suit changing market conditions and circumstances, the elevated level of employee churn, which was already high in more "normal" times, has introduced accelerated conveyer-belt workplace discontinuity and associated corporate amnesia. These are modern phenomena that have prevented institutions from learning from their own hard-won and expensively paid-for experiences. The result? A never-ending recital of repeated mistakes, re-invented wheels, and other unlearned lessons, the cost of which is significant. By any measure, the attendance of unremitting and poor determinations by employees on behalf of their employers signifies the matching forfeiture of their own special acquired "wisdom"—and this book's title.

By reducing the level of poor decision making in a clearly identifiable quarter of corporate dysfunction, employers will help to address the late Peter Drucker's declared crisis of productivity, his belief being that businesses and other types of organization are largely wasteful in their production. This book will outline how, through two misconceived and underexploited processes of KM, employers can learn to work more efficiently, even *with* high employee churn. The processes are the better management of their Organizational Memory (OM) and proper employer-instigated Experiential Learning, the use of which will also enable organizations to continue utilizing the experiences and acquired wisdom of employees *after* they have left their employer's employ. And by addressing the limitations of conventional approaches to decision making and Experiential Learning, this book takes KM to the next level with the biggest big-ticket application of all in today's economic quagmire. By way of repetition, productivity has a very, very close relationship with competitiveness and that elusive prize growth....

Keywords

wisdom, growth, competitiveness, Experiential Learning, Knowledge Management (KM), Organizational Memory (OM), productivity growth, decision making, human resources, The Learning Organization, flexible labor market, job continuity, corporate amnesia, continuous improvement, knowledge transfer, knowledge preservation, action learning, after-action reviews, innovation, business education, experience, corporate history, economic history, cliometrics, case studies, exit interviews, oral debriefing, explicit knowledge, tacit knowledge, Experience-Based Management (EBM), lessons learned, repeated mistakes, reinvented wheels, hindsight, evolution, disenfranchise, benchmarking, mentoring, Brazil, Russia, India, China, and Korea (BRICK), MBA

Contents

Author's Credentials ix

Preface xi

Chapter 1   The Race Where Every Sprinter Drops the Baton 1

Chapter 2   Getting from A to B Without Going Via Z 11

Chapter 3   Here Today, Gone Tomorrow....................................29

Chapter 4   Opportunity Knocks for Business Education 39

Chapter 5   "I Forgot to Remember!" 57

Chapter 6   The Smart March to Wisdom 79

Chapter 7   How the Baton was Passed 97

Chapter 8   Way to Go 103

Appendix: Checkbooks and Boxing Gloves: Origins of the
Author's Interest 107

Notes...113

References 123

Bibliography..131

Index 135

Author's Credentials

Arnold Kransdorff was the first to identify the phenomenon of corporate amnesia in the early 1980s, soon after the flexible labor market started to make a significant impact on job tenure. His first book on the subject, *Corporate Amnesia*,[1] was short-listed for the United Kingdom's Management Book of the Year in 1999 and was selected as one of 800 titles worldwide to launch the Microsoft Reader eBooks program in 2000. His second book, *Corporate DNA*,[2] expanded the subject to explain how organizations could help their transient managers apply captured knowledge and experience in the cause of better decision making. This edition updates the subject even further.

An expert practitioner of Knowledge Management (KM) and the leading authority on the consequences of the flexible labor market, his unique specialty is the management of Organizational Memory (OM), the institution-specific know-how accrued from experience that characterizes any organization's ability to perform. His work is widely published in academic journals, trade journals, and the national press. He has project managed and edited over a dozen corporate histories—the most efficient vehicle for capturing long-term OM—and pioneered the development of oral debriefings—the equally efficient verbal vehicle to capture short- and medium-term OM.

A former financial analyst and industrial commentator for the *Financial Times* in London, he has won several national and international awards, among them Industrial Feature Writer of the Year (1981) and an Award of Excellence (1997) from Anbar Management Intelligence, the world's leading guide in management journal literature. He has co-supervised a U.S. doctoral thesis on OM, is a guest lecturer at many U.K. and overseas business schools, and is a regular speaker at international business conferences. He has assisted in the Royal Society for the encouragement of Arts, Manufactures, and Commerce's Inquiry on Tomorrow's Company, the Economic and Social Research Council—commissioned study on Management Research, the Confederation of British Industry's deliberations on Flexible Labour Markets, and the

Washington, D.C.—based Corporate Leadership Council's study on New Tools for Managing Workforce Stability.

Contact: ak@corporate-amnesia.com (+44) 01923-896288 or (m) (+44) 07906-059435 or through www.pencorp.co.uk & www.corporate-amnesia.com

Preface

This updated third edition takes a fresh look at the discipline we know as Knowledge Management (KM), first launched on an enthusiastic academic and business world out of a small Boston conference in 1993. Predicated on the belated realization of the premium value of knowledge, the gathering of a handful of academics and practitioners came about because of two overlapping developments in the way business had changed: globalization, which had brought greater complexity to the marketplace, and the ubiquitous computer. Attendees thought the latter could help the former.

Since then, universities have started courses on the subject, journals have grown up around it, and many large organizations have invested in it. It is a multi-billion dollar market, often seen as a must-have and then, after the installation of some very expensive digital machinery, misapplied as just document management in place of hard-copy file storage.

By the serious practitioners, it is linked to human resource management and incorporated with processes such as *The Learning Organization, the information age, continuous improvement, transactive memory systems, knowledge transfer, action learning, and after-action reviews,* among others. Typically techno-centric through electronic data systems, its employment is sometimes tied to organizational objectives, such as improved performance, competitive advantage, innovation, the examination of corporate culture, and developmental processes, but its practice is still uncertain— just like its multiple definitions. In universities, academics are mostly validating and still teaching early theory, whereas out in industry and commerce, serious practitioners (of which there are still relatively few) are at sixes and sevens with the concept and its practice. In truth, knowledge management is still an immature discipline, begging for a bigger and better role. Academics and so-called specialists know it is important, the chests of money they are spending on it make this clear. But they do not know why exactly or, in the modern lingua franca, how to make it "rock."

With just two decades of the subject's development in train, the KM tag has become a useful way to describe how to share data, information and knowledge within and across institutions, an endeavour that is now recognized as key to making industrial and commercial headway in the complicated marketplace, now even more complex by growing globalization. It also has a defining role in helping to get the developed world out of the all-enveloping economic quicksand already closing in.

In practice, industry and commerce have imaginatively applied technology towards creating big—and expensive—ways of preserving their corporate records with a view to getting relevant data and information to the right people at the right time. That is the theory. Trouble is, according to academics that have researched this objective, few decision makers efficiently utilize this amazing resource.

The reasons are unclear. Possibly there are the time constraints under which managers find themselves. Egotism is another possible reason, a characteristic widely deemed necessary for executives that encourages them to feel that their instinct and education know better. Elsewhere, prior data and information as well as experience is not seen as being anything more than dry "history," a discipline with no sticky connection between yesterday, today, and tomorrow. More likely, though, decision makers don't know how to properly *apply* their employer's tried and tested experiences, whether they (the experiences, that is) be successful or unsuccessful, remembered or forgotten. The operative word is apply, where individuals should, the theory goes, consider coupling their own know-how with the institution-specific knowledge gleaned from their employer's experience and turn it into new knowledge applicable to changed circumstances. The discipline is known as Experiential Learning, self-evidently learning from their own and others' experience, the original perceived role of KM. In its old, unstructured format, it was known as learning the lessons of history.

More recently, *Experiential Learning* has been interpreted by educationalists as blending theory and practice. The premise is that students complement classroom instruction with hands-on activities; they learn by doing. At one end of the spectrum, Experiential Learning for the Santa Cruz Waldorf School's eighth-grade class is to put students through a "ropes course" using simple games and more complex, active problem-solving initiatives involving scenarios and dangerous missions. It mirrors the outward bound courses that many organizations undertake to engender bonding and problem solving. At the other end of the spectrum, Experiential Learning is the use of internships and other types of apprenticeships, while students at Canada's Acadia University can join an on-the-job co-operative research and development program with private industry. At Australia's Charles Sturt University, the process allows nurses and clinical science students to engage in problem-based or scenario-type learning. For others, it is touring museums or offering students educational opportunities at foreign universities to address spreading globalization.

But real Experiential Learning goes much further. The concept's starting point is that individuals or organizations seldom learn from experience unless the experience is assessed and then assigned its own meaning in terms of individual and/or the organization's own goals, aims, ambitions, and expectations. From these processes come insights and added meaning, which is then applied to new circumstances, the product of crafted wisdom. The end product is better decision making.

To make Experiential Learning work properly—that is trigger the "apply" component of the process—requires a special skill, firstly the ability to synthesize *relevant* and *available* data, information, knowledge, and experience with another, even more rare, quality. This is the supposed ability that turns a decision into an added-value decision, that difficult-to-define capacity to marry an action to the changing environment in a way that is anything but prescriptive. Obscure and seemingly consummate, it defines the manager, it is his/her's raison d'être and the quality that justifies their bigger bucks. As such, and as this book will explain, it is better learned rather than taught. For want of a better description, it is the ability to enact that perceptiveness that is called enlightenment or, better, wisdom.

In truth, industry, commerce and academia have been short-changing the way it has been building KM in pursuit of this elusive attribute. The discipline is still a misnomer, more like document management, because, excluded from the sophisticated data banks is a key component of the knowledge necessary for the acquisition of this wisdom. Coupled with this, employers are not specifically enabling decision makers to convert their data and information into knowledge and then into new knowledge. And finally—or rather primarily—industry and commerce are still not adequately addressing the equivocal downside of the workplace phenomenon known as the flexible labor market, the modern-day development responsible for scattering an organization's "wisdom" every which way but in the direction of the organization that created it. Fortunately not all arrivals and departures are synchronous, so there is an element of experiential overlap in the workplace, but it is still reasonable to conclude that, at any one time since the flexible labor market started in earnest in the early 1980s, employers have been working with virtually no medium- and long-term memory of their own making. For every successive generation of employees since then—around seven in some countries—the organization's previous short-term memory will also have disappeared, leaving no establishment with *any* corporate inheritance to speak of.

The bottom line is that, no thanks to the flexible labor market, industry and commerce have become exclusively dependent on the skills and experience of their short-tenure employees and then *their* short-term replacements, and so on. Businesses have, by default, elected to disregard a major proportion of their available source of wisdom engendered by their *own* prior experiences that, because they are already tried and tested in their own environment, are infinitely more valuable.

When organizations *DO* find the flexible labor market *too* flexible— that is when demand exceeds supply, either through skills shortages, natural or enforced wastage—most of the corporate effort is devoted to trying to reduce the level of departures, usually by improving salaries and/or perks. When this doesn't work, or if it only works partially, the conventional wisdom is to take a deep breath and keep looking in the belief there is nothing else they can do, at least in the short term. As the record shows, the prevailing remedial measures do little to stem what has become a very flexible market. The truth is that there *IS* something else institutions can do.

The supposition of this book is that however much industry and commerce see it as an unalloyed godsend, the unaddressed flexible labor market is the biggest single impediment to the acquisition and application of institution-specific wisdom and good decision making. To continue to benefit from the advantages of the flexible labor market, organizations need to bring back their disappearing wisdom by better managing their Organizational Memory (OM), what is effectively the detail of the what, why, how and when of institution-specific experience. This book shows more of the *why* they should do it, and then—through an approach called **Experience-Based Management (EBM)**—*how* they can do it, with some unique features that address the limitations of traditional KM approaches to improving decision making, namely:

- It introduces and clarifies the term "Organizational Memory." Although other related terms are more frequently referred to (such as institutional or corporate memory, corporate experience, or even corporate/management history), the use of this lexicon is deliberate. Most other KM processes cheerfully claim to apply individuals' "memory." However, the memory used does not generally utilize anything other than current practice, no thanks to short jobs tenure. For full-on Experiential Learning to be efficient, the evidential base should include *all* experience: both current and prior, institutional, personal, and where possible, others' experience, the concept otherwise known as benchmarking. For the agnostics who argue that prior experience is irrelevant because circumstances change, this text's retort is that this is illustrative of a pervasive misunderstanding of how organizations mainly learn and progress. They do so *organically*—and not just within narrow timeframes. The fact that conditions are always changing is *exactly* why it becomes useful. Decision making is not a reflex skill, and the lessons derived from prior experience are an abstract dress rehearsal for real decisions to come. Thus, if education's erudition is truly valued, the awareness of prior experience, especially organization-specific familiarity, is more beneficial than its ignorance. In essence, its cognizance should not be misinterpreted as a pretext for repetition, for the key to better decision making is in the *application* of OM. The designation used is to more accurately define OM in the context of Experiential Learning and decision making.
- It directly tackles the negative consequences for employers of the flexible labor market and, even when employees do not move on, individuals' inherent short, selective, and defensive memory, by incorporating a practical (and cost-effective) way

of capturing short-, medium-, and long-term experiences before they are lost forever. The processes described make the organizations' evidential base permanently accessible to the rolling generations of managers. Instructively—and surprisingly—corporate amnesia is hardly acknowledged, let alone addressed, by many KM practitioners.

- It incorporates into the wider learning process a part of intellectual capital (arguably the most useful component) that is often overlooked. The customary input is explicit experience and knowledge, the type of data, information, and old knowledge that is likely recorded in an institution's digital data bank and/or is available elsewhere. This approach describes the means by which the more elusive and valuable *tacit* knowledge and experience can be captured and incorporated into a learning model.

- As a general rule, KM's conventional applications are to concentrate on avoiding or dealing with mistakes. The EBM model focuses on decision making as a tool to improve on both success and failure.

- Finally, EBM uses Professor David Kolb's reflective process to formulate a distinctive *"lessons learned"* approach to decision making that can be passed along the short-lived generations of employees. It should be stressed that the mechanics of academically-authenticated Experiential Learning à la Kolb, whose methodology is Experiential Learning's most refined process to date, has *not* been tinkered with, save for adapting it to the modern workplace.

This is the subject of this book, a text that shows how organizations can also take advantage of their second-hand experience, their third-hand experience, and so on. It's a multi-skilled application called EBM involving, firstly, the efficient capture of identifiably important short-, medium- and long-term OM and particularly the tacit knowledge contained therein, the methods of which are explained. Covering all important corporate events, other big decisions and random episodes that recur, this must happen before memories become blurred and/or key employees walk out of the front door. Thereafter, with the evidence in hand, successive generations of employees must know how to apply their new employer's OM alongside their own and others' recalled experience in order to address new circumstances. Then, using Kolb's model adapted to the modern workplace and the unique and distinctive "*lessons learned*" approach of EBM, the outcomes can be passed along the short-lived generations of employees.

This text also explains why good decision making needs to shift away from being based on a generic one-size-fits-all skill to an institution-specific competence that employers have to coordinate themselves by making all of their experience available to their transient employees. It additionally provides business education and industry/commerce with a formalized, improved, practical, inexpensive, and continuous methodology with which to teach business and commerce's most important competence. And it takes the Cinderella model of KM to the next level by helping to take decision making out of the land of practiced guesswork.

CHAPTER 1

The Race Where Every Sprinter Drops the Baton

Progress, far from consisting in change, depends on retentiveness. When change is absolute there remains no being to improve and no direction is set for possible improvement: and when experience is not retained, as among savages, infancy is perpetual.
—George Santayana, US philosopher and poet[1]

When the London Olympics was staged in July/August 2012, bosses all over the world will have had the opportunity to see an aspect of management they themselves neglect in the way they make, and are taught to make, their decisions. Over much of the 64-year period since the event was first staged in Great Britain's capital, athletes were using a technique that enabled them to achieve performances way beyond administrators in industry and commerce. While athletes' attainments have consistently improved since the late 1940s—in fact the progression in their scores has never been faster in all history—managers in OECD countries have presided over declining rates of both productivity and productivity growth over most of the same period[2] (see Figure 2.1, Page 12 and Figure 2.2, Page 15). The discomforting paradox of the timeframe is that the athletes' measure is only slightly longer than the availability of widespread business education.

Alongside superior diets and full-time training schedules, the athletes were using a technique called ***Experiential Learning***, self evidently learning from experience, in their case via the medium of movie film and video of their own and others' performances. Through the recorded evidence of prior practice, they had been *applying* their own and others' knowledge and experience, out of which has been extracted the so-called "wisdom" needed to create new knowledge that addresses new circumstances.[3] In contrast, managers in industry and commerce have been largely short changing the wider concept when it comes to how they make their employer's determinations; in fact, organizations have been consciously and energetically pursuing a workplace practice that is actually *discarding* their own acquired wisdom. The institutions aside, the culpable party is the much-vaunted flexible labor market, otherwise known by its outcome—short jobs tenure.

It is around this phenomenon, its consequential effect of imposing widespread workplace discontinuity, corporate amnesia, and the process by which wisdom is classically acquired that there is much misunderstanding, even of the difference between knowledge and wisdom.

Wisdom is an obscure quality, often equated with intelligence, being smart, gifted, being intellectual, and/or scholarly. Yet its manifestation is not necessarily dependent on *any* of these attributes. It has a special property—good judgement, a feature that probably explains the business success of so many of the unschooled. And because judgement of any sort cannot be arrived at in isolation, a necessary component of the journey is knowledge and actual experience, both one's own and others'. In the world of business, and because it is the most relevant, this includes—crucially—the *employer's* knowledge and experience. It is the soundness of an action or decision that defines this rare quality and on which depends most progress.

To fully understand wisdom's nature, it is necessary to comprehend the precise character of all the components of this terminological marathon. By way of illustration, the announcement of a company's annual results, on its own, is data while a comparative relationship with, say, a previous performance figure becomes information.

In contrast knowledge[4] is interpretative and predictive, it is a deductive character allowing its owner to understand the implications of data and information and act accordingly, the action becoming experience. Knowledge is described in different ways: by Alvin Goldman[5] as justified true belief, by Bruce Aune[6] as information in context, by Verna Allee[7] as experience or information that can be communicated or shared and by Karl Wiig[8] as a body of understanding and insights for interpreting and managing the world around us.

A separate and transformative task, the component that adds value to knowledge and experience is wisdom. Without it, the action—that is the ensuing decision—becomes no more than repetition in a new time frame. In fresh contexts, where circumstances are always different, triumphs can easily be forfeit. What is evident, then, is that the continuing ability to acquire wisdom is a required element for survival in a competitive world and an equally obvious component in the way managers are taught how to learn to make good and better decisions.

The confusions that often arise around these clarifications are various, one of the biggest being the muddle between the nature of the acquired wisdom of individual employees and the organizations for which they work. In truth, the wisdoms are separate, interconnected, and reliant on each other's unique physiognomies. Without each other—for example when the employee moves on—both become disassociated. And while employees can theoretically passage their "memory," however remembered, to a new employer, the source organization is typically left in oblivion. Where understandings fall down is when employers mistakenly believe that the imported experiences of replaced individuals—even high achievers—substitute for an organization's already tried-and-tested experience.[9] To be effective, imported experiences still have to be *adapted* to a new employer.

Non-interchangeability of experience can also be seen in the example of a taxi driver, whose basic skill is driving. Driving, though, is not universally applicable, because a New York taxi driver will have to learn another type of driving—left-side driving—to earn a living in the U.K. Equally, the additional street and traffic knowledge that makes the New York taxi driver a better New York taxi driver is quite irrelevant in London. The logic is deafening. One decision-maker, however good in one situation, is not necessarily of the same quality in another, however similar the occupation is. Decision making is environment specific.

Elsewhere, among those who acknowledge that circumstances **DO** always change, there are those who believe that an organization's prior experience is of little or no use—despite businesses visibly acknowledging the contrary by paying more for experienced employees. One argument, already indicated, is that it is just history, a discipline with no sticky connection between yesterday, today, and tomorrow.

With those who have moved on from this paradigm, some believe it is only short-term experience that is important. Because of its contemporaneous nature, it may have an edge, but knowledge is not time-specific when it comes to the art of good management and decision making. Elsewhere, many businesses consider that it is only their mistakes that warrant educative attention; in truth, successes can also be improved upon. Then there is the naïve belief that one or two retained old timers are sufficient for the recall of *all* experiences. Knowledge—yet others imagine—is, anyway, embedded in their expensively constructed data banks, in which is recorded the company's written records. However, useful and necessary to good decision making is the provision of generic data and information, the contents are usually passive and, as a physical or digital resource, widely unheeded anyway.[10] Excluded is the type of knowledge central to the acquisition of wisdom.

By way of further explanation, knowledge is made up of an explicit component, sometimes called skilled knowledge, and tacit *or* cognitive knowledge, also known as "coping skills."[11] The former is the type of knowledge such as the professional or vocational skills that are recorded in the abundant manuals and textbooks and offered up in training courses, what this author calls the "what" of know-how. Tacit knowledge on the other hand is the non-technical "how" of getting things done, what has been called "operacy"[12] or "techne"[13] (Greek for "skill") and what this author calls the "how" of know-how. Much of it is implicit, ambiguous, and certainly esoteric, and acquired largely by experience that is functional and, in its most instructive forms, context-, co-worker- and institution-specific. Typically existing in the minds of individuals, it is normally very difficult to capture. But it is through tacit knowledge that most erudition takes place, where old knowledge is transformed into new knowledge with the added value variously called hindsight, insight, 20:20 vision, good judgement, enlightenment, having the quality of being sensible, and—the holy grail—wisdom.

At this point it is instructive to point out the differing perceptions towards knowledge in general. The broad belief in the West is that it is mostly technological and/or quantitative in orientation.[14] Western rationalism is based on the theory that knowledge comes through deductive reasoning while Eastern empiricism reasons that erudition is derived inductively through actual experience.[15] As Experiential Learning specialists Professors Ikujiro Nonaka and Hirotaka Tekeuchi confirm, managers in Western economies generally focus on technically-orientated, mainly explicit information-encompassing rules, processes and the professional/vocational information codified in manuals and texts, while the emphasis in Japanese companies, for example, is on the more implicit and ambiguous tacit knowledge, a characteristic that is deeply rooted in action as well as ideals, values, and emotions. It is part of their Zen Buddhist heritage and culturally helps in the Japanese way of change.

In the world of decision making, the difference—in exactly the same way as many managers mistake information management for knowledge management—is as subtle as it is important. As an essential part of the evolutionary process of applying prior experience to new circumstances (in Nonaka and Tekeuchi's words *"turning old knowledge into new knowledge"*), tacit's importance is barely acknowledged by Western managers. Few will even know how to define it, let alone show any concern when it walks out of the front door.

For the acquisition of wisdom and good decision making, the academic label for the journey is experiential learning, a discipline which—surprisingly—is also short changed when it comes to teaching managers how to better make their employer's determinations. MBA teaching is not exempt, despite an apparent scholastic belief in the model's utility. Conventional business instruction is largely a one-size-fits-all education that is designed to provide generalized skills within specific fields such as finance, marketing, strategy, and leadership. Formal business education tries to accommodate their own interpretation of Experiential Learning through mediums such as universal case studies while employers use stratagems such as apprenticeships, induction, and—at management level—storytelling. Other more sophisticated attempts at keeping pace with innovation and workplace adaptation include disciplines such as Action Learning and Change Management. Using outdoor pursuits such as climbing, snow-shoeing, white-water rafting, and dog sledging, some practitioners also put Team Building under the umbrella of Experiential Learning.

While these approaches go some way to accommodate the narrower interpretation of Experiential Learning, employers and educators still largely overlook a bundle of related and new issues that compromise established learning strategies, of which the above-mentioned are just a few. The overriding oversight—the flexible labor market—is the much-prized development of modern business with a long-term outcome that seriously devalues the short-term benefits, explained as follows.

In the first 30-odd years between the two London Olympiads— that is the immediate post–WWII years—most employees could expect to have one or two, and if they were really unlucky three, employers in their working lifetimes. With personnel across the workforce—including managers—now having an *average* eight different paymasters[16] in many countries, employee tenure is around five years, effectively up to 20% shorter if one takes into account lower-output induction periods, notice times, and intervals of unemployment. While the commonplace high rate of jobs churn undoubtedly enables employers to more quickly adjust to changing circumstances, there is a hidden downside—high workplace disruption and a low level of institutional memory exacerbated by individuals' inherent short, selective, and defensive recall abilities.[17] This, in turn, hides a misjudged consequence for employers—the phenomenon of corporate amnesia, which manifests itself in the pandemic of repeated mistakes, re-invented wheels, and other unlearned lessons that litter modern industry and commerce. To continue the Olympic metaphor, it is the business equivalent of the relay race, where each sprinter drops the baton. To further emphasize the potentially devastating impact of migrating employees, academics have estimated that up to 90% of the knowledge in any organization is embedded and synthesized in peoples' heads.[18] Simply stated, the recently departed means that, for employers, most of their special knowledge and related wisdom goes walkabout, never thereafter available for use by its instigator. This diminishes the effectiveness of prevailing learning strategies, which mostly only have *recent* experiences to work with.

The fact that there is often some experiential overlap in the high churn rate is providential but it is still reasonable to conclude that, at any one time since the flexible labour market started in earnest in the 1980s, employers have had access to declining levels of medium-and long-term memory of their own making. For every successive generation of employees since then—around seven in many countries—the organization's previous short-term memory will have disappeared, leaving no establishment with *any* employer inheritance to speak of. With only one generation's short-term memory to work with—the contemporary one—is it any wonder that the corporate beneficiaries of short tenure have a legacy of short-termism? And why, these days, can one decade's sector leader very, very easily be another decade's laggard. And, for employers, there's the trillion-pound question for academics to study using Thomas Malthus and David Ricardo's law of diminishing returns in mind:[19] Is lots of second-hand experience really better without much accrued organizational-specific wisdom?

What has happened is that employers have removed themselves from much of the more relevant and, arguably, the most important form of practice from which to learn—their institution-specific experience that, otherwise, could be shared with resident employees. By institution-specific experience, this text is referring to organiza-tions' ***own*** tried and tested experience, what this author has designated as their Organizational Memory (OM) and which allows them to build on their already tested successes and failures. The precise raison d'être for this is that every organization is unique to itself and that most progress is organic.

To put all this into an educational and corporate context, blue-collar skills are generally predicated on available explicit knowledge while white-collar administrative skills are grounded in the less-than-visible tacit knowledge. Explicit knowledge can be taught but tacit knowledge is best learned. For business-type decision making, the distinction is palpable. Teaching is instruction received while learning is instruction acquired out of an abstracted process of critical reflection, reasoned deduction, and applied action, the evidential base for which is OM. Truly, for employers to expect decisions to be made without reference to OM and, specifically, their tacit knowledge is—to use more athletic imagery—hamstringing management.

More simply stated, without the better management of homegrown OM, the best that institutions can do is learn from the outside experiences of replaced employees, another of the professed values of the flexible labor market. While this undoubtedly gives organizations access to new blood, new enthusiasm, and new experiences, this always depends on the replacement individuals' worth; it should be noted, however, that others' experiences are not always relevant, remembered accurately, truthful, or even transferrable. This poor interchangeable value of experience has been supported by three Harvard Business School academics,[20] already indicated (see Page 3).

The consequential lost productivity is enormous, a picture that can be drawn from the already-mentioned declining rates of per capita productivity growth in OECD countries since the 1950s (see Figure 2.2, Page 15) when, bizarrely, business education has never been more accessible. And while it is difficult to apportion any shortfall *solely* to poor decision making from corporate amnesia, a further indication of the extent of the problem is one big management consultancy's estimate[21] of the broad cost of wasted productivity in several major OECD countries—between 5.9% and 9.7% of their GDP (see Table 1.1).

So, no thanks to the flexible labor market, industry and commerce have become exclusively dependent on the skills and experience, however remembered, of their short-tenure employees. Employers have elected to disregard much of the other available source of wisdom, their own experiences that, because they are already tried and tested in its own environment, are infinitely more valuable. The picture is even more graphic if one likens most prior experience in the context of the flexible labor market to the immortal words of John Clees in his dead parrot sketch: *"E's not pinin'! 'E's passed on! This parrot is no more! He has ceased to be! 'E's expired and gone to meet 'is maker! 'E's a stiff! Bereft of life, 'e rests in peace! 'Is metabolic processes are now 'istory! 'E's off the twig! 'E's kicked the bucket, 'e's shuffled off 'is mortal coil, run down the curtain and joined the bleedin' choir*

Table 1.1. The Cost of Wasted Productivity

	Cost (US$ billion)	% of GDP
Germany	266.1	9.7
Spain	84.0	8.1
America	888.8	7.6
Britain	158.5	7.5
France	121.3	5.9

Source: Proudfoot Consulting, September 2005.

invisible!! This is an ex-parrot!!!!" So much for institutional experience and its embedded wisdom!

To quote timeworn and more relevant independent understandings of whether or not to address this new workplace issue, consider the illustrative dialogue in English novelist J. L. Carr's 1972 book *Harpole Report*:[22] "*You have not had thirty years' experience. You have had one year's experience 30 times.*" Alternatively, ponder what Professor Robert Hayes, ex-IBM and McKinsey, told a Harvard Business School audience in 1984:[23] "*In the pure and physical sciences, each generation inherits the conquests made by its predecessors. But in the moral sciences, particularly the art of administration, the ground never seems to be incontestably won.*" Finally, consider the advice of J. G. Pleasants, a former vice president of Procter & Gamble: "*No company can afford the luxury of rediscovering its own prior knowledge. Understanding the company's past can lead to adapting previous successes, avoiding old mistakes and gaining knowledge far beyond personal experience.*" Significantly, all were conveyed before flexible working was such a large entry in the corporate lexicon.

In this author's own experience, there are few conscientious employees, and especially retirees—from senior managers downward—who do not have any important and/or relevant institutional wisdom to impart. Alongside most ranks of employees, one of the most prolific individuals was the departing departmental secretary of a large pharmaceutical company.

So, how can organizations' nomadic wisdom be rescued and/or taught?

To be able to take full advantage of their prior experience—and the flexible labor market—employers need to be able to continually work with their short-term memory as well as the memory beyond the average four/five years of experience to which commerce and industry have sentenced themselves. Managed properly, today's OM can become the wisdom for tomorrow and the day-after-tomorrow's managers to stop repeating organizational mistakes, to improve on successes and not to have to re-invent already-won wheels. "*I forgot to remember*" is an excuse that needs to be its own distant memory. And because no one else can provide them with their own OM, it is up to employers themselves to orchestrate the resource.

Short jobs tenure, corporate amnesia, experiential non-learning, and poor decision making are all now inter-related phenomena of the modern workplace. To better benefit from their flexible workforces, employers need to make much better use of their dormant wisdom that, manifestly, has already been hard-won and expensively paid for. Whispered another way, it is an approach that maximizes human capital by utilizing employees *after* they've left the premises, an enticement for nil-cost gain if there ever was one. And the derivative opportunity for educators is that industry and commerce need to be better taught how to learn to do it—and all for one big fat additional reason: to help improve productivity, the lifeblood of competitiveness, and the key to staying in the game. Not the type of productivity that comes from just labor cutbacks and capital retraction, but the more serious productivity that can be understood from the title of the next chapter—Getting from A to B without going via Z, the time-honored formula that kick starts the ability to sell more. If one can sell more, *ipso facto* growth....

Take the latest economic crisis, the most serious since the 1930s with costs in the trillions to the power of plural. At the time of writing, the predicament is more than four years old. The heavy-handed fiscal and monetary measures have, as yet, brought little gain and the prospect is for many more years of austerity. How to cut the heavyweight deficit *and* realize growth is the desperate new religion. Given that most economists see productivity increases as one of the main factors to trigger economic growth[24] and that the agreement of Eurozone countries in 2011 was that the resumption of growth had to come through a relentless focus on improving competitiveness,[25] why, then, is not active, dedicated and real Experiential Learning loudly on the training schedule? Much like those very fit Olympian contestants.

And just to check whether or not this might work, consider this: deep as the United States' problems are, which developed country is showing the most growth? The United States, whose productivity still tops all its competitors!

CHAPTER 2

Getting from A to B Without Going Via Z

The urgency of the productivity challenge is great. The country that does this first will dominate the twenty-first century economically.
—Peter Drucker, management guru[1]

He has been portrayed as the man who invented management,[2] a testimonial borne out of his sage-like predictions of many of the major developments of the century in which he lived. The description, which appeared in the trade journal *Business Week* in the month of his passing in 2005, when he was 95, listed how he had foretold the advent of privatization, decentralization, the rise of Japan to economic dominance, the importance of marketing, and the beginnings of what he called the information society with its requisite for lifelong learning.

Fourteen years earlier Peter Drucker, a financial reporter, groundbreaking management consultant, award-winning author, and a respected teacher spanning six decades, made another prediction of even more substance about an issue that has been on the minds of industry and commerce for as long as businessmen have thrown their money at investments; how to turn the unit of one into more than one, a process otherwise known as productivity? Witnessing that industry and commerce were largely wasteful in their production, Drucker said bluntly that the urgency of the productivity challenge was *"great.*[3] *The country that does this first will dominate the twenty-first century economically. Unless this challenge is met, the developed world will face increasing social tensions, increasing polarization, increasing radicalization, possibly even class war."*

Drucker's keen judgment and visionary challenge was evidence based. Although the developed world had provided the greatest ever improvement

Percentage annual average growth

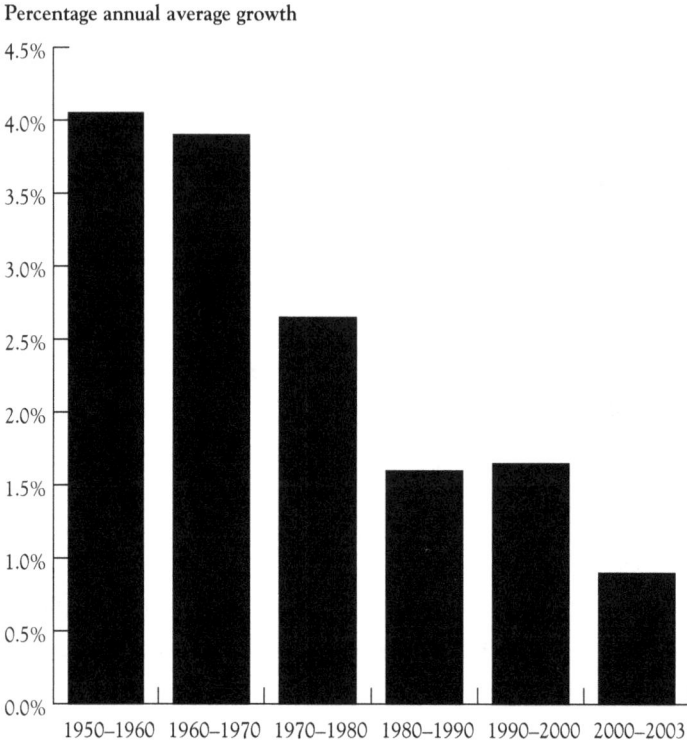

Figure 2.1. OECD's productivity growth 1950–2003.
Source: Groningen Growth and Development Centre and the Conference Board, Total Economy Database, August 2004, http://www.ggdc.net

in living standards over the 20th century, the level of *productivity growth* has been waning.[4] By way of clarification, *productivity* is the output produced per unit of labor, usually reported as output per hour worked or output per employee.[5] *Productivity growth* is the increase in output not attributable to growth inputs such as labor, capital, and natural resources and is driven by technological advances and/or improvements in efficiency.

Of all the number crunching that organizations do to evaluate their performance—from gross margins, return on capital employed to market share—the productivity measure is probably the most accurate indicator of policy-making and decision-making skills. As such, its computation is more a gauge of management rather than just labor. Mischievously, and given the growth of management levels and numbers within the workforce, it is tempting to suggest that it should be expressed in terms of output per unit of *management*.

This aside, productivity improvements over the long term are the main contributor to rising living standards, otherwise called wealth. When productivity growth declines, the ability to compete weakens. When productivity growth falls into the red, it means that businesses are getting less than added value from their endeavors. New investment in many areas makes little sense and margins become increasingly difficult to achieve.

For their profits, employers' first instinct is to then increasingly depend on a reduction in inputs such as employees, raw materials, and capital. The usual area this comes from is workers, the reduction of which automatically affects the quality of service and/or higher prices. And when price increases are not supported by real productivity, that demon, inflation, kicks in. Thenceforth, when higher prices are not supported by corresponding higher value to the consumer, the result is a further loss of competitiveness and a downward spiral to bankruptcy.

Productivity's importance is critical in several ways. In addition to the end-of-Chapter 1 assertion that productivity improvement is the as-yet unemployed approach to combating the current credit crunch and recession, it is the ability to do things efficiently, and particularly more efficiently than others, that, at the end of the day, determines wealth. In bull-market times, productivity is often seen as less than compulsory but when the bear rears its ugly head—as it is doing at the moment—productivity's solicitation is generally seen in terms of cutbacks. Enabling competitiveness, it is also one of the main requirements for businesses *staying* in business.

In the latest pre-recession years, management emphasis had been to maximize the efficiency of capital investment, specifically in technology. These tactics, however, have now virtually played themselves out. Workers employed in making and moving things accounted for a near majority of employees in the 1960s, whereas they now number less than one-fifth of the typical workforce, meaning that there are now too few employees in such jobs for their productivity to be decisive.[6] Employee numbers have been squeezed to the point where, Drucker said, the human element of doing business has seemingly become almost mechanical. While interest rates in many developed economies had come down from the high levels of the early 1990s, the capital factor was so big that providers were demanding shorter-term returns. And although technology improvements look endless, the initial momentum that it provided for savings was ebbing quickly.

All this is serious enough for individual companies but what happens when whole countries lose their edge?

Using productivity figures before the latest recession, which has temporarily distorted and upset most countries' economic performances, the United States has held the top position for much of the 20th century and, even today, is way ahead of the Organisation for Economic Cooperation and Development (OECD) pack by a significant margin. With a few exceptions, mainly the countries that have come up from a low economic base, the rest are mostly struggling (see Figure 2.1, Page 12) to inch ahead. The inside story *across the board*—including the United States—is one of declining annual growth rates, indicating that the developed world is fast running out of steam.

The average productivity growth figures for 2000–2004[7]—a more normal period of marked global growth—showed that, among OECD countries, Italy, Luxembourg, Holland, Spain, and Switzerland had moved into negative territory (see Figure 2.2, overleaf). And the rest's average annual growth was a paltry 0.8%.

How productivity impacts on competitiveness can be seen by the same source's 2003 figures, which showed, for example, that it cost more in France than in the United States to perform similar tasks; in France, the outlay was lower than in the United Kingdom; in the United Kingdom the cost was less than in Spain; and in Spain, the cost was lower than in New Zealand. The difference between the United States and New Zealand was more than 40%, confirmation of the United States' premier position in the productivity, competitiveness, and wealth stakes, an indicator of productivity's variety and the potential for improvement among the laggards.

In the multifaceted world of productivity, this untrumpeted collapse—now more serious as a result of the subsequent global slump—is a late warning sign of systemic trouble for developed-world industry and commerce. It (reinforced by Drucker's challenge) is also an eleventh-hour alert that has been threatening for decades, with all remedial measures

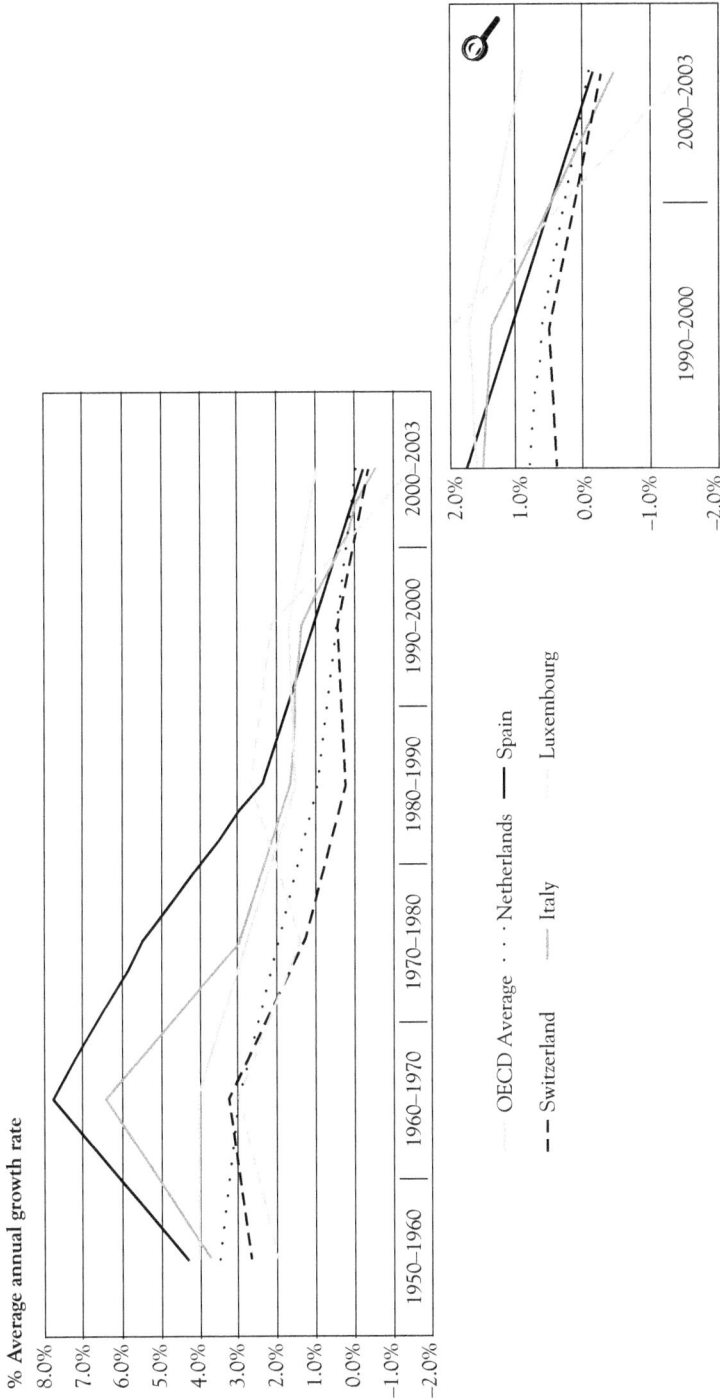

Figure 2.2. **Productivity growth not sustained.**
Source: Groningen Growth and Development Centre and the Conference Board, Total Economy Database, August 2004, http://www.ggdc.net

giving the patients only provisional respite. The significance of these figures is that this was the first time in modern industrial history that productivity momentum had reversed among so many developed economies at the same time and with so many others in stalling mode. It is the business equivalent of crashing through WWII's Maginot Line, the fortifications erected on the eastern border of France; considered impregnable, it was easily flanked by the Germans in 1940.

Painting an even more graphic picture of the situation, the domestic trains are running out of steam, at less than a quarter of the average rate it did in the 1950s. The United States, the first-class ticket holder, is travelling at slightly more than half the pace, with almost all the second-class ticket-holders at crawler speed, while Luxembourg, Italy, Holland, Switzerland, and Spain are in reverse gear.

Obviously a serious issue for policy makers, productivity carries a curious misunderstanding that can be seen in the knee-jerk responses of many businesses and, in particular, governments in the provision of their public services. To them, improved productivity is mostly directly related either to cutbacks, usually in the form of redundancies, or to the provision of more working capital/higher budgets. For example, the research by international management consultants Proudfoot, out of which emerged Table 1.1 (see Page 8), divulged that the majority of senior executives—55%—thought that the key to raising productivity was to increase investment, with no specific mention of doing things more efficiently. In the United Kingdom's case, it was suggested that the Government was aiming very low in its bid to boost productivity growth and that it had its sights on the wrong targets. The results, incidentally, were assessed in a fat year, 2005.

To improve productivity, many governments also see their role in improving the macro environment for business by, for example, giving business more agreeable tax incentives, introducing subsidies, import duties, and interest rate adjustments to improve export prospects, reducing red tape and/or contributing to improving training facilities, the use of which generally affects competitiveness rather than productivity. These measures are clearly expedient but, as history shows, they have brought only temporary respite.

The history of productivity makes the problem clearer, showing how productivity ebbs and flows in broad timeframes. Its past performance has been uneven across both countries and industries.[8] The United Kingdom held the top slot for most of the 19th century with an annual productivity growth rate of 1.2% from 1820 to 1890.[9] In the 20th century, the laurels went to the United States, with an annual growth rate of 2% from 1913 to 1989. From 1950 to 1973, it was Japan's turn; its productivity increased by a factor of almost six, which resulted in an 8% annual rate of productivity growth.

If one can understand Ireland's latest defaulting position, it is the Emerald Isle that has been the most impressive performer from the lowest base over the longest period of time; over four decades, its productivity growth averaged an impressive 3.4% a year, closing the productivity gap with the United States from 37% to 89% by 2003. When compared with the United States over the same period, the other most improved OECD countries have been Australia (from 68% to 78%), France (64% to 86%), All Germany (60% to 71%), Italy (from 54% to 75%), Japan (from 34% to 71%), Spain (from 35% to 65%) and the United Kingdom (59% to 74%), all of which have been losing ground since 2003. The worst performer was New Zealand, its productivity gap widening in three shallow waves from 80% in 1965 to 58% in 2003, with Holland's divergence against the United States virtually unchanged at 70% and latterly static.

On both competitiveness and productivity growth,[10] the average EU economy receives worse ratings than the United States and the group of other OECD economies in every area bar social inclusion. As a general rule, weak and mediocre performance is country-specific while high performance is issue- or organization-specific. In the global picture, industries like manufacturing, farming, mining, construction, and transportation have shown an annual increase in productivity of 3%–4% over the last 100 years. These performances are the clearest indicators of how good (and bad) have been various nations and their industry sectors at learning from their own and each others' experience.

It should be noted that Armageddon is not being predicted just yet because the major industrial countries do not compete with each other in the same way corporations do. They are, for example, each other's main export markets and each other's main provider of useful imports. Also, calculating productivity—like all number crunching—is an imprecise science, especially with international comparisons that typically involve judgements by human compilers and self-protective politicians. The wider picture moreover depends on which formula and database is used. For example, OECD figures based on "per-hours worked" record that negative growth rates have been recorded several times in various countries at different times over the past 30 years.[11] However, using "per-person" figures adjusted for countries' living standards, which arguably provides a clearer picture of underlying reality, the current picture looks distinctly wintry.

To back the stated observations, this text is using the authoritative Groningen dataset[12] derived from underlying information in the OECD's Structural Analysis database, which, in turn, is derived from national sources. Groningen applies the Elteto-Köves-Szul method of calculation (these figures used its latest 1999 EKA $ rate), which is a measure of exchange value that permits direct comparisons between economies. Called "purchasing power parity" (PPP), they differ from standard market exchange rates that are influenced by short-term capital movements by measuring direct price level differences between countries. This is done by directly comparing the prices of similar goods in different countries. For example, they convey how much a euro would buy in London or in New York, allowing the figures to reflect living standards. A good example of a PPP-type measure is the Economist "Big Mac Index."

Normally, small changes in data comparisons are not significant but the flagging growth figures extrapolated from Groningen's productivity databases are not just isolated to the early 2000s. The downward drift is evident over a 40-year period, closing with the negative scores in the five mentioned developed countries at the same time. The wider trend can also be clearly corroborated in other databases.

The point is that overall productivity growth among many developed nations is now dangerously low and the upside prospects that might come from pipeline products in the form of nanotechnology's molecular manufacturing and genetic engineering are still a decade or so away. With timing considered everything in business, it is going to be an uncomfortable ride for many until these factors kick in. In the competitiveness stakes, China, for example, is looking very threatening, as is India, Brazil, Russia, and Korea, the so-called BRICK countries that many forward-looking investors have designated as prime investment areas. For these fast-learning emergents, the overtaking opportunity has never been greater, for the aspirants also host one of the other most valuable of all commercial needs—captive markets that span more than one third of the world's population.

Drucker's productivity challenge is instructive in other ways. His reference to service workers includes government and the civil service that today represents an enormous sector of the economies of most countries and which does little or no manufacturing or other forms of production. As a general rule, productivity in this sector is lower than private industry—often substantially lower—and mounting pressures to deliver better value services are now requiring public administrators to also become better decision makers. And although Drucker was referring specifically to developed countries, his challenge is no less relevant to countless emerging economies, many of which have aspirations to leap into the modern world without the experiential advantage of their predecessors or, in many cases, without the desire to learn from others' experience. Like their First World cousins, the aspiration to also learn from their own experiences appears just as remote.

The big question for both the experience-rich and the experience-poor is who is going to learn faster?

In any argument, it is important to provide good evidence for the conclusions—in this case how flexible working can affect productivity at the coalface. Aside from anecdotal substantiation (see Chapter 5), which is voluminous, there are several good examples that uphold the supposition. One study[13] that does this looks at the cost of knowledge loss, which can otherwise be categorized as corporate amnesia. A team of U.S. academics computed the impact of what they called the *"forgetting phenomena"* on the learning life cycle of skilled manual tasks in a manufacturing plant. Using actual learning data on more than 60 individuals undertaking the same task, they imitated the effect of forgetting by subjecting their learning life cycle to a series of interruptions, which, in practical terms, could be directly equated with workplace discontinuity. On the basis that many activities have been described by cyclic models such as the product life cycle and organization life cycle, the researchers reasoned that the same approach would apply to the performance of a task, where each phase of the task could be described as part of a task "life cycle." Subjecting their learning cycle model to an interruption after 12 weeks over a 50-week period, their calculation was that project performance could be expected to retrogress to 52% of optimum output.

A second study comes from the Washington-based Corporate Leadership Council,[14] which put the percentage cost of jobs change at 46% of annual pay for frontline employees, 176% for IT professionals, and 241% for middle managers. These included direct expenses associated with replacement hiring and training but also, significantly, the lost productivity associated with a vacated position and the lost productivity of peers and subordinates. Elsewhere, the U.S. actuarial and consulting firm Segal Company calculated that in specialty retailing, for example, which incurred a 90% annual turnover rate, it costs half of the industry's total earnings to deal with the problem.[15] A retail store would have to sell 3,000 additional pairs of khaki pants at $35 apiece to overcome the loss of one worker, it said. Replacing a manager or professional costs much more. It suggests that employee turnover in the United States may double in the next economic recovery.

Some of the unseen costs of staff churn were the subject of another study[16] by a Californian management and training consulting firm specializing in employee commitment and retention. Among several of its Australasian clients, they found that employee turnover was costing a 400-plus employee IT services provider more than NZ$16 million a year. Across the Tasman Sea, staff turnover at an 18-employee beauty aids manufacturer and distributor cost more than NZ$2 million in lost sales opportunities annually while the equivalent figure for an 80-store supermarket chain was at least NZ$40 million.

One other interesting study[17] by the United Kingdom's National Westminster Bank disclosed that more veteran companies in the United Kingdom failed in the early-1990s recession than in any other previous economic slump in the 20th century. A massive 10% of firms that had survived two world wars, the bleak 1930s depression, and the succession of subsequent cyclical downturns crashed between 1989 and 1993. Why were they unable to survive this particular recession? Part of the answer—to this author at least—lies in the fact that the recession coincided with the height of the downsizing boom. This led to massive jobs discontinuity and a situation that provided individual companies with little awareness of how they maneuvered their way out of previous crises. No actual figure was placed on the collective effects of all these corporate deaths.

These examples also endorse the universal understanding that almost all learning—whether personal or corporate—is evolutionary, incurred incrementally from the building of one experience on top of another. This helps to create a framework of reference points from which to make informed judgments and help to refine decisions. When the process is interrupted, for example by workplace discontinuity, the learning cycle erodes. Progress, then, has to resort exclusively on the *School of Hard Knocks*, the idiomatic description of learning from new negative experiences and, truthfully, a somewhat repetitive and wasteful way of procuring erudition when the experiences may already have been expensively tried and tested.

While these example might help to persuade organizations that flexible working is not all positive, the ongoing picture is, as already shown, not exactly rosy, with productivity growth scores collapsing alongside the recession's less-than-helpful effects.

To work out how to dig oneself out of the hole, it is perhaps enlightening to look at productivity in several other ways.

The way business is done has changed fundamentally. For most of the years to the 1970s, the developed world concentrated on making and moving things, a workplace that was populated by blue-collar workers.

In this period, the cost of almost all employees (except management) was always considered too high, hence the deliberate shift to technological alternatives to production. The trouble with this move was that the reallocation of resources was illusory in many industry sectors due, no doubt, to underlying social and political considerations led by demand and inflation. Wages continued to rise, often in excess of inflation and in many cases out of step with productivity. The effect was not to diminish the relative weight of labor in the production computation; instead, labor's substance continued to be a key factor—often the most important constituent—in the workplace. Then, knowledge working started to change the profile of the workforce just as flexible working arrived to disrupt jobs continuity and drag in its wake the single biggest encumbrance to decision making excellence—institutional memory loss, otherwise known as corporate amnesia. With its unquestionable impact on productivity and competitiveness, the flexible labor market and its co-conspirator corporate amnesia is—bizarrely—still an unacknowledged factor of production.

In that period much of the effort to improve productivity was directed towards making processes and manual workers more efficient, mainly through business-speeding technological advances. Today, the nature of the workplace is more service orientated, requiring a large part of the workforce to be knowledge centered. This requires a completely different emphasis towards productivity.

Unfortunately, managers' mindsets have not changed much, still focused on the idea that the responsibility for productivity improvements rests with the "workers." Unfortunately, the relationship of productivity to these approaches is tenuous without the ability to do the same things more efficiently. In efficiency's absence, the result is just higher-than-needed levels of capital or lower-than-necessary levels of service.

On the basis that there is not much more to squeeze out of current manual workers, this book's submission is that the emphasis has to shift towards non-manufacturing occupations and, even more importantly, managers themselves. Based on the recent historical record that their determinations are conferring virtually no upside potential for their employers, it is *they* who have to improve their decision making qualities. It is a conclusion that gets corroboration from Drucker, who says that it is managers, not nature, economic laws, or governments, that make resources productive,[18] a view also confirmed by McKinsey Global Institute (MGI), whose research[19] into the manufacturing sector shows a strong correlation between national productivity rankings and management practices.

Taking the argument further, it is useful to look at productivity in yet another way, specifically at a side of industry that has shown exponential progress, discover why and then apply their solution more generally. In the scientific sector, for example, an area whose development over the past 100 years has been nothing short of spectacular, star players have included aircraft and automobile developments, radio, transistors and television, medicine, nuclear power, computers, and the Internet. More specifically, there are now stem cells to cure diseases, photonic crystals for superfast optical computer chips, nanotubes for electronics, quantum cryptography for secure communications and a biochip that uses water droplets as tiny test tube. Who would have thought them possible a decade ago?

Their extraordinary rate of innovation and progress is down to one unique dynamic that differs from other subdivisions of industry. Their evolution—that is the wider subject and/or individual product development—has been virtually seamlessly incremental, the building of one advance on another.

In contrast, there is little "evolution" in the world of decision making, the organisations' most important skill on which is dependent everything from product quality to profitability and continued existence. As the record of unlearned lessons show, process is rarely examined inclusively, continuously, or effectively. Alongside this, the actively pursued flexible labor market has effectively removed all prior institution-specific experience bar the first-hand understandings of the most recent incumbent employees. Even if they wanted to, organizations today have not generated the relevant and useful internal resources to fully examine and learn from their own experiences. In truth, all they've got to work with are the experiences, however remembered, of other organizations provided by *their* replacement employees, an explanation for the pandemic of repeated mistakes, reinvented wheels, and other unlearned lessons that litter many parts of modern industry and commerce.[20]

Whatever the rate of employee turnover, it would appear that managers have, anyway, innately short, selective, and defensive memories. For conceptual advocacy, there is a substantial body of academic research to support this.

Harvard scholar Alan Kantrow[21] observes that *"when we go to work, we forget."* To Kantrow, managers' choices and actions may find a ready place in memory, but the reasons and the intended significance of their deeds quickly float out of reach and beyond recall. He observes that while all organizations have some form of recall, their memory is frequently inaccurate: *"The style of a business presentation, the kinds of evidence that tend to sway decisions, the shared sense of what constitutes relevant information about a new market or product, the deep-seated visceral preference for certain lines of business—all these characteristics, and a thousand others like them, are the subtle products of memory. In no two organizations are they exactly the same, nor in any two parts of the same organization. Intuitively we know this. But on the job we usually disregard it. In particular individuals forget both the density and duration of the activity underlying the surface facts. We forget that, like an iceberg, nine tenths of the mass lies hidden, well below the normal waterline of vision. And we forget that the part we can see is not just 'there' but is very much something built, something constructed or pieced together over time."*

For confirmation that outlines the unwillingness of many companies, mainly Western organizations and their managers, to objectively examine their decisions, especially their mistakes, Harvard's Professor Chris Argyris[22] explains that whenever a manager's performance comes under scrutiny, the individual begins to feel embarrassed, threatened, and because they are so well paid, guilty: *"Far from being a catalyst for real change, such feelings cause most to react defensively. So, when their learning strategies go wrong, they become defensive, screen out criticism and put the 'blame' on anyone and everyone but themselves. In short their inability to learn shuts down precisely at the moment they need it the most."*

This is explained as a particularly well-developed managerial ego. Commenting on the difficulties of teaching managers how to learn, Thomas Barry,[23] a top U.S. industrialist describes the apparent amnesia evident in many of his top employees: *"For many years I have been troubled by the inconsistent attitudes of high-achievement professionals who have superb intellects yet appear not to learn from experiences or colleagues."* His explanation is that companies attract *"the stereotypical self-motivated, supercharged MBAs whose past successes build their defenses against being incorrect, hence against any need to learn or change."*

This author's additional explanation[24] (difficult to academically prove, however) is that in business education and in industry/commerce—and indeed wider society—individuals are socialized to encourage insecurity in the belief that it will generate fewer mistakes. As individuals' defensiveness shows, it also discourages individual learning—the antithesis of the desired result—a condition that, in practice, reduces the skill of much decision making to little more than intuition, untested judgment, political expediency, subjective thinking, experimentation, and delay. Put differently, it is guesswork coupled with the ability to play the game of corporate politics well.

Alongside the observation of Professor Roger Hayes mentioned earlier (see Page 9), what these academics and businessmen are confirming is that there is something inherently prejudicial in the way decision makers make their determinations, more specifically that whatever progress the above-mentioned science sector has realized in recent years, the achievements have been *despite* managements' best efforts. More profoundly, their observation suggests that there is something missing from business education.

If, then, the likes of Drucker, McKinsey, Argyris, Kantrow, Barry, Hayes, and others can be believed, the way to become more productive is for business to look towards non-traditional ways to improve decision making, specifically employing a methodology that helps managers address remembering, their inability to examine their performance objectively and continuous learning. As other appraisals of educational shortcomings will show in subsequent chapters, such an approach starts to look suspiciously like David Kolb's reflectively orientated model of Experiential Learning adapted to some mechanism that anticipates the knowledge loss from workplace discontinuity.

Drucker's shorthand is for organizations to *"work smarter,"*[25] the catchphrase first coined by the American industrial engineer Frederick Winslow Taylor[26] more than 125 years ago. Best remembered for developing stopwatch time analysis, which combined with Frank and Lillian Gilbreth's later methods[27] to evolve into the field of time and motion study, Taylor was a mechanical engineer who sought to improve industrial efficiency, the 19th century term for 20th century productivity. Later, their efforts evolved to become "human relations"—HR—thanks to Harvard Business School's Professor Elton Mayo's work in the electrical industry.[28] Their approaches, which were mainly top-down—that is manufacturing workers were *told* how to make improvements—took a quantum leap after WWII when it was realized that workers themselves might have views on how their productivity could be improved. Out of these collaborative approaches came new methodologies such as Total Quality Management (TQM),[29] quality circles[30] and Douglas McGregor's "Theory X" and "Theory Y,"[31] all imposed on the back of the other stimuli to productivity—capital, new technology, and job cutting. As Drucker has acknowledged, their and others' contributions were, indeed, unique and impressive, providing much of the productivity increases for the manufacturing worker in the 20th century.[32]

Coincidentally, all were exceedingly good examples of Experiential Learning in their own right.

While Taylor used a timepiece on manual laborers, Drucker's way of working smarter was to identify a completely new category of business activity and its unstructured experts—knowledge workers.[33] They were the people who operated primarily with information or who developed and used knowledge in the workplace, now a huge business sector estimated to outnumber all other workers in North America by at least a four to one margin.[34] Crucially, it was these workers whose productivity Drucker considered to be the next frontier of management.[35] Given that much production would move away from the developed world to the cheaper developing world, the identification of this new category of business was logical but the way Drucker said this *should* happen—through continuous learning and teaching—is the instructive element alongside his five principles of effective knowledge work. Coincidentally, almost all of them are identical to the role of managers generally, namely the need to build effective teams, to communicate, to create, share and maintain knowledge, to align one's time with strategic goals and negotiate next steps.

Explains Drucker:[36] *"Capital cannot be substituted for labor. Nor will new technology by itself generate higher productivity. In making and moving things, capital and technology are factors of production. In knowledge and service work, they are tools of production. The difference is that a factor can replace labor, while a tool may or may not. Whether tools help productivity or harm it depends on what people do with them, on the purpose to which they are being put, for instance, or on the skill of the user."* Redesigning a job and then teaching the worker the new way to do it cannot by itself sustain ongoing learning, he says. *"Training is only the beginning of learning. Indeed, as the Japanese can teach us (thanks to their ancient tradition of Zen), the greatest benefit of training comes not from learning something new but from doing better what we already do well."*

Like most evolutionary efforts, this was the seed of the next-generation approach to improving productivity, although commerce and industry seem still stuck with the old idea that the source of such gains is primarily the people who make and move things.

The kernel of the work of Drucker and some of his contemporaries was in also seeing managers, whose stock in trade was also with data and knowledge, as knowledge or service workers. His "learning" and "teaching" can be understood to be the empirical component of David Kolb's next-generation Experiential Learning, with managers being responsible for "creating" and "maintaining" knowledge in their employer's context. Drucker's "learning," then, was the application of prior experience in the cause of good decision making and teaching was the "sharing" of the subsequent acquired wisdom with the next generation.

This suggests that the approaches to improving productivity by businesses and, in particular, governments in the provision of public services, have to change. And for this to happen in the era of low jobs tenure, companies and other institutions have to better manage their migrating source of evidence known as Organizational Memory, a rarified type of data, information and knowledge that is institute specific.

CHAPTER 3

Here Today, Gone Tomorrow

We learn through experience and experiencing, and no one teaches anyone anything. This is as true for the infant moving from kicking to crawling to walking as it is for the scientist with his equations. If the environment permits it, anyone can learn whatever he chooses to learn; and if the individual permits it, the environment will teach him everything it has to teach.

—Eric Hoffer, U.S. philosopher[1]

Organization Memory (OM), sometimes called institutional or corporate memory—or even history—is the company equivalent of individual DNA, which is often described as the blueprint of an organism or the molecule of heredity because parents transmit copied portions to their offspring.

Much the same can be said of OM. It is the accumulated body of data, information, and knowledge created in the course of an individual organization's existence. Like DNA, it has inheritance potential in that, because its content is tailored to the organization's unique business activity and way of working, its record of tried-and-tested experiences is a hereditary source of valuable knowledge for on-going application. Put another way, it provides a decision-making rehearsal, out of which can emerge the more rigorous ability to make determinations for a future that will be just a little more familiar. Falling under the wider disciplinary umbrella of knowledge management (KM), it has two repositories: organizations' archives, including electronic databases, and individuals' memories.

This book will not be directly concerned with archives as they exist in their traditional format, a function that is primarily a physical/mechanical/ digital utility that incorporates the collection, classification, storage of

corporate documentation and other texts. It typically comprises all inter-
nally generated documentation relating to an organization's activities, the
record of intellectual property (patents, copyrights, trademarks, brands,
registered design, trade secrets, and processes whose ownership is granted
to the company by law, licensing and partnering agreements), the details
of events, products, and individuals (including relationships with people
in outside organizations and professional bodies) and relevant published
reference material. Consisting largely of so-called explicit knowledge, this
is a function that is well trodden by generations of skilled archivists and
now by very imaginative information technology (IT) professionals.

Important as conventional archives are to learning and the decision-making function, it is the other, less accessible component of
OM that this text tackles—the esoteric, mind-resident knowledge and
experiences which are subject to innate memory lapse and departure
as a result of the flexible labor market. It is the part of the organization's intellectual capital that greases the corporate wheels, that which
has been paid for at great expense and which, puzzlingly enough, is
readily discarded. It is also a factor of production—arguably the most
important—that organizations neglect to address. It is *tacit knowledge*,
the event-specific, organization-specific, person-specific, and time-
specific "how" of know-how, the other descriptions of which—along
with those of data, information, explicit knowledge, and experiential
learning—have been outlined in Chapter 1. Its significance in the quest
for wisdom and decision making excellence can be illustrated by the
11 narrative words of the Strategic Planning Director of the Australian
airline Qantas:[2] *"We're overrun with information, but we're dying for lack
of knowledge."*

At this point it is useful to describe some actual examples of tacit knowledge's singular character and its importance as a decision-making tool.

The first comes from David Snowden, former director of the
Knowledge and Differentiation Programme at IBM Global Services. He
uses the analogy of how best to get around London's roads. One could use
a map, which contains information with which to navigate using universal
symbols and structures to observe, orientate, and then decide how to
move. But using the services of a cab is faster because the driver uses his
tacit knowledge compulsorily acquired over 30 pre-qualification months

cycling round the streets of London. To this could be added the tacit knowledge gained from day-to-day experience of changing bottlenecks and throughways.

Another example of tacit knowledge comes from New Zealand KM specialist, Carl Davidson.[3] Davidson's pen picture is: *"Remember how Grandma baked the best scones you've ever eaten? Maybe you've got her recipe but no matter how many times you've tried, your scones never turn out as good. In reality Grandma, by writing down the recipe, only gave you explicit knowledge. What you also need is her tacit knowledge—how she worked in the butter and milk, how she kneaded the dough. Conventionally you would get this by talking to her face to face, watching her or making a batch beside her."*

Two other examples refer to the Qantas-like dilemmas of the National Aeronautical and Space Administration (NASA) and the United States' atomic bomb program. As one would expect, both were particularly well documented—that is their explicit knowledge was comprehensive, recorded, and accessible—but lacking in a certain, special way that, on their own, would not be sufficient for later use.

According to a NASA official: *"If NASA wanted to go to the moon again, it would have to start from scratch, having lost not the data, but the human expertise that took it there last time."* [4] This was exactly the reason for the people who constructed the United States' atomic bomb to undertake what they called the Knowledge Preservation Project at Los Alamos, where the bomb was born.[5] In the wake of the U.S. Government's decision to stop testing nuclear weapons, there were concerns that the skills developed would atrophy, so, in the event that it had to one day resume testing, and perhaps actually use the weapon, retired weaponeers were brought back to the laboratory for video-taped interviews intended to salvage knowledge about nuclear bombs that could not be gleaned from blueprints and archived documentation. Researchers recorded more than 2,000 videotapes. The rationale of John D. Immele, the then director of nuclear weapons technology at Los Alamos, was, *"We don't want to press the erase button on our memory and go back to where we were 50 years ago."*

What Los Alamos was, in fact, doing was collecting as much of the tacit knowledge as they could to rebuild the past without having to re-invent it. And even if they were not aware of it at the time, they were also providing the evidence with which they could build a better product in a much shorter timeframe and also cheaper. The implications for companies and other organizations are great. For countries, the collective repercussions are even bigger.

Yet another example belongs to BP in the United States, whose interest in experiential learning came about when a group of Ohio employees solved a dangerous butane leakage problem that had gone unnoticed by managers for eight years. The fact that its efforts in this direction did not prevent the company's repeated safety mistakes in other areas is discussed in Chapter 5, one possible explanation being that knowledge sharing was not extensive enough.

To solve the butane leakage problem, BP hired researchers from the Massachusetts Institute of Technology to produce a so-called learning history.[6] Using oral debriefing techniques (which this author/practitioner has further adapted in his own methodology) interviewees recalled their experiences anonymously and in their own words in a way that reflected their collective learning experience. The transcripts were then used to extract insights that become a best practice manual that managers and staff read before starting another project of a similar nature and which personnel specialists are using to design training. The technique is said to have saved £22.5 million in a three-year trial at just one of its refineries. Dozens of other efficiency projects and two learning histories have been launched at the refinery, helping staff to increase productivity—says BP—by 35% in a two-year period. Paul Monus, who launched BP's first learning history at the Lima refinery in Ohio, is apparently advising other refineries how to introduce the techniques of oral debriefing. Projects have taken between three and nine months to complete and cost from $10,000 to more than $150,000, the larger ones involving up to 100 debriefings and 2,000 pages of narrative.

One other similar project was undertaken at Ford,[7] which debriefed 1,200 employees tracking the progress of teams in the United States, Hungary, Ireland, and Brazil in a car parts division, at an assembly plant, and in product design and development. Vic Leo, a systems dynamics and organisational learning manager at Ford in Detroit, estimates that the assembly plant factory has achieved quality improvements of 25% a year since 1995 compared with less than 10% achieved for two comparable factories. "*The plant was ranked third out of the three when we started. When we stopped our learning history it was number one."* Among its benefits, says Leo, the learning history helped expose unexpected problems such as culture clashes and knock-on effects on other systems when a new working practice was spread throughout Ford's 380,000-strong workforce. He dismisses traditional consultancy reports—they can put *"too much of their own spin on a story"*—as formulaic. *"Often you read reports about teams which are filed away and forgotten. But the learning histories captivate the readers. I also feel they give a much rounder picture."*

For the purposes of good decision making, it is instructive to understand that once knowledge is documented, it reverts to being information. New knowledge—what some academics call knowledge in action[8]—is created between the interaction of experience, explicit knowledge, and tacit knowledge, either incrementally[9] (one experience on top of another), accidentally,[10] or through innovation.[11] The former is the usual way knowledge is created, incremental and accidental being atypical and rare, although innovative can always work in conjunction with incremental.

The reality is that even though most organizational work processes are largely designed around documentation, much remains unrecorded, especially that to do with the key practical skill of decision making. Also, the typical documented record often reflects the desire to gloss over disagreements and serious questions, especially mistakes.

For the purposes of this subject and for OM to have any use at all for its source organization, the tacit component of knowledge needs to be recorded in some way in these times of high jobs turnover.

In truth, the nature of tacit knowledge is widely misunderstood.

Normally unstated, it is often associated with intuition and, as such, rich in the "how" of know-how, the very practical way of getting things done in an employer's unique circumstances. It encompasses deeply entrenched beliefs, ideals, values, and mental models, all of which dictate a personal—and derived corporate—way of doing things. As a general rule, however, individual owners and organizations are completely unaware of it or of its value to others. On their own, they also find it difficult to recognize, isolate, document, and even verbalise.

Thereafter, there are many misconceptions surrounding it, mainly because only a small number of professionals have seriously tried to capture it.

In the field of KM it is typically believed to be difficult to share with others through both the written word and articulation. The best way of conveying it, they believe, is through extensive personal contact or social networks.[12] In fact, the understanding is that an individual can acquire tacit knowledge without language. Apprentices, for example, work with their mentors and learn craftsmanship not only through language but by observation, imitation, and practice. As such, tacit knowledge can only be acquired through practical experience in a relevant context.[13] Without some form of shared personal experience, then, it is extremely difficult for people to share each others' thinking processes.

All this is largely accurate but now, in today's new workplace, basically irrelevant and uninformed. The point is *not* that tacit knowledge can't be shared except through personal contact. The flexible market doesn't *allow* much—or any—sharing. And the Los Alamos Knowledge Preservation Project and BP's Learning History, mentioned earlier in this chapter, show that tacit knowledge *CAN* be documented and shared, as this book will show in a way that accommodates the new workplace.

In truth, the workplace has changed out of all recognition. It is now much more "flexible." Whilst there is no accepted definition of the phenomenon, it has a number of common characteristics, they being contractual flexibility, wage flexibility, occupational flexibility, and geographical flexibility. The accepted political wisdom is that this is an economically beneficial development, hence the efforts by governments of most persuasions to enable their countries to become as lithe as possible. The organizations that endorse and encourage the flexible labor market include the companies themselves, their trade organizations, governments, even bodies like the OECD and the European Union. With the possible exception of trades unions (usually for self-interested reasons), they all classically think that the alternative, the acquisition of other employers' experiences—that is external hiring when necessary—will cover any potential downside consequences. Just how ingrained the flexible labor market has become can be seen in the attitude of the various stock exchanges around the world, which have become addicted to companies cutting jobs to enhance earnings.

The rationale is persuasive: because of the changing nature of the marketplace, businesses need to be able to adjust their workforce numbers or hours worked quickly and without too much expense, circumstances that have necessitated fewer regulatory constraints. The critics say that flexibility puts all the power in the hands of the employer, resulting in an insecure workforce. Conveniently, few ever think of computing the true price tag.

While acknowledging both points of view, this text does not seek to challenge this development directly except to observe that it appears to address only short-term considerations. Yes, the absence of regulatory restraints on employment is generally beneficial to an employer but the actively encouraged flexible labor market also serves a more long-term and inhibiting handicap. It imposes widespread workplace disruption and an Alzheimer-like—also iceberg-like—corporate amnesia that disallows organizations the ability to benefit from their own hindsight.[14] This ensures that institutions can't efficiently evolve incrementally, which is the way most organizations progress. These outcomes are among the largest contributors to decision making weakness, productivity shortfall and lack of competitiveness.

To gauge how much "knowledge" walks out of the front door, it is instructive to look at the various country levels of employee churn. Because of the latest recession, the levels have, inevitably, been distorted negatively but it can be reasonably concluded that whatever the past staff turnover rate, levels are now higher than before.

Some historical staff turnover figures have already been signposted in Chapter 1. There is a wide discrepancy between official figures and independent research, but even at official 1998 levels for example, (see Table 3.3, overleaf) most developed countries have breached the point at which, at least one company, BP, considered its 11% staff churn to be sustainable.

Following the beginnings of the flexible labor market in the 1980s, the rate escalated sharply due to downsizing and then has varied with individual country circumstances as the phenomenon became a general feature of the labor market. Among those countries with accepted flexible labor workforces, the trend is such that few businesses or other organizations have *ANY* employees *in situ* beyond very short periods of time.

By 1983 the United States' National Bureau for Economic Research reported[15] that the average American employee would work for 10

Table 3.1. Average Tenure (Years)

Country	1992	1995	1998
Belgium	11.0	11.3	11.6
Denmark	8.8	8.5	8.5
Finland	–	10.7	10.6
France	10.4	10.7	11.3
Germany	10.7	10.0	10.3
Greece	13.5	13.4	13.2
Ireland	11.1	10.8	10.1
Italy	11.9	12.1	12.1
Japan	10.9	11.3	11.6
Luxembourg	10.1	10.6	11.2
Netherlands	8.9	9.1	9.4
Portugal	11.1	12.3	11.6
Spain	9.9	9.9	10.0
Sweden	–	10.6	11.9
United Kingdom	8.1	8.2	8.2
United States	6.7	6.7*	10.5
Average	10.2	10.4	10.5

* Data refer to 1996.
Source: Eurostat, Statistical Office of the European Communities, and national aggregate data from the United States and Japan.

different employers during their working life times. By 2000, the annual average turnover rate was 16%.[16]

By the early 1990s, the United States headed the world discontinuity league[17] (see Chapter 4, Page 50 for an explanation of how America contradicts the core argument by being better experiential learners), followed by Denmark, the United Kingdom, Holland, Spain, Ireland, and Finland. Since these rankings were published, overall job tenure further declined, in some geographical areas quite markedly. In the United Kingdom, for example, the number of different employers that new entrants to the labor market would have over their average 44-year working lifetime was estimated to be 11,[18] in 1997 down to eight,[19] in 1998 giving organisations average of around a four-year tenure for their employees. By 2001, labor turnover was 25%[20] on a year-on-year basis. This churn was equally evident in the boardroom, the average tenure of Chief Executive Officers in British blue chip companies being just 4.6 years.[21] More than a third of these CEOs were in office fewer than two years and a further 30% left the boardroom within four years. Just one in 10 stayed for a decade or more. The respected London-based Employment Policy Institute[22] forecast in the same year that new entrants to the workplace could expect to have an average 11 different employers in their working life times. Later figures[23] find that one in three workers now remain in their jobs for less than two years whilst one in five considers changing employers in the first 12 months of their new employment.

Further down the corporate ladder, the outlook is just as volatile. According to even more recent research,[24] more than two thirds of workers were looking through the Internet's social network sites to move away from their current employers. A total of 40 percent were researching prospective employees and 32% were actually applying for jobs.

Consider, then, the outcome for organizations then, now, and tomorrow? No medium- or long-term memory, with just a soupçon of the short-term.

But there is something else happening in the wake of the actively encouraged flexible labor market, with potentially more serious consequences. With the relationship between knowledge and power intimately linked, the corporate body has, quite deliberately and entirely unwittingly, allowed its command to be displaced,[25] challenging flexible working's critics. No longer are individuals an aggregate *part* of an established institution. Individuals *are* the institution for as long as they remain *in situ*. Then, when the face changes, as it is doing on average every four or five years in many developed economies, the institution changes, or more accurately, tries to change, bereft of its continuity and at the mercy of new brooms. Ordered evolution has become a shapeless revolution with little regard for the one corporate asset that represents the organization's life form—its institution-specific knowledge and experience. It presages a mercurial world, with such things as corporate culture, ethos, values, and tried-and-tested usage struggling to maintain an even keel. Having chosen to operate in isolation to its *own* hard-won and expensively acquired experience, the motor of much of western society's wealth machine has largely disempowered itself. This book does not suggest that the flexible labor market should be abandoned as a workplace strategy; it has some extremely valuable features. It is proposing only that the better management of OM and use of proper experiential learning will help to counterbalance the evident institutional disenfranchisement to give productivity its much-needed fillip.

The theory is that business education should serve business needs, so, what did business education and its market—employers of almost every description—make of the near 30-year-old phenomenon of the flexible labor market, Peter Drucker's 20-year-old declared crisis of productivity, and David Kolb's four decades of developing experiential learning in the curriculum?

CHAPTER 4

Opportunity Knocks for Business Education

The palest ink is better than the best memory.

—Chinese proverb

At first glance, the 20th century's development in life-style improvement is remarkable, more impressive than in any other century, at least in the developed countries. Some of the advancements have been outlined in Chapter 2 and undoubtedly much of the progress is directly attributable to political choices. But at the practical level, the momentum has unquestionably derived from the world of business and in turn its managers, suggestive of a keen ability in the field of decision making.

In turn, the theory goes that much depends on the quality of available business education, an argument that would be irrefutable but for the evidence[1] (see Figure 2.2, Page 15) that managers in developed countries are turning in productivity growth scores that are lower than their untutored counterparts in the 1950s and 1960s—and the long list of credible business people and academics that decry the prevailing system of how the next generation of decision makers are schooled.

A random selection of remarks from academic research studies and other sources is instructive and deliberately extensive to demonstrate this author's attempts to be objective and not too selective or politically correct. It also presents business education with an opportunity to help solve several of the workplace's newly created problems that threaten to disempower the established wealth machine.

- **Professors Henry Mintzberg and Joseph Lampel:**[2] *"Of the four American CEOs people most often named when asked who had accomplished great things, none had a business school degree* *and two—Galvin of Motorola and Gates of Microsoft—didn't even finish college."*

- **Professor Jeffrey Pfeffer and Christina Fong:**[3] *"Possessing an MBA neither guarantees business success nor prevents business failure."*
- **Professor Gary Hamel:**[4] *"Most of the best ideas in management over the past decade or so did not originate in business schools."*
- **Professor Harold Leavitt,**[5] on business's premier qualification: *"We have built a weird, almost unimaginable design for MBA-level education that distorts those subjected to it into critters with lopsided brains, icy hearts, and shrunken souls."*
- **Professor Robert Hamada,**[6] ex-dean of the University of Chicago's business school, on the MBA: *"The industry is overbuilt."*
- **Richard R. West,**[7] ex-dean of New York University's graduate school of business, on management school research: *" …. fuzzy, irrelevant, and pretentious."*
- **Professor J. S. Armstrong,**[8] a 30-year MBA teacher: *"In today's prestigious business schools, students have to demonstrate competence to get in, but not to get out. Every student who wants to (and who avoids financial and emotional distress) will graduate. At Wharton, for example, less than one percent of the students fail any given course, on average …. the probability of failing more than one course is almost zero. In effect, business schools have developed elaborate and expensive grading systems to ensure that even the least competent and least interested get credit."*
- **Professor Robert Buzzell,** Harvard Business School:[9] *"The mark of a true MBA is that he is often wrong but seldom in doubt."*
- **Academic research:**[10] *"Business schools are not a major source of books that directly influence management thought, whether measured by sales or by more subjective assessments of the value of the books."*
- **Academic research:**[11] *"The research done in business schools only makes a modest contribution to management practice and management thought when compared with research produced*

by non-academics such as journalists, consultants, and people working in companies."

- **Allen Yurko**:[12] US chief executive of Siebe, one of United Kingdom's top 50 companies by market capitalisation, on Britain's managerial abilities, in 1997: *"The U.K. is one of the most difficult places in the world to turn on the growth switch. Industrial managers in Britain lack the skills at expanding their businesses. The U.K. is an excellent place for manufacturing but on the whole UK managers are downsizers. They are restructurers and wonderful at it. This is necessary but at some point you need to grow."*
- **Professor John Adair**,[13] Exeter University, on the United Kingdom's managerial abilities: *"Any leaders Britain does have are a result of accident, not design."*
- **Professor Michael Porter**,[14] Harvard University, on Britain's poor showing as a generator of wealth: *"It stinks."*
- **Anita Roddick**,[15] founder and managing director of Body Shop International: *"Business schools dampen entrepreneurship."*
- **Sir Bryan Nicholson**,[16] a former chairman of the Post Office and ex-head of the Manpower Services Commission: *"When you compare Britain's adult workforce, from top management down, with those of our main competitor countries, we emerge as a bunch of thickies."*
- **Lord Young of Graffam**,[17] former Secretary of State for Trade and Industry under Margaret Thatcher: *"For all too many years people went to schools which despised the world of work and went to universities which totally rejected it."*
- **Council for Excellence in Management and Leadership**,[18] created in 2000 to develop strategies for educating U.K. managers: *"Current management and business leadership development is a dysfunctional system."*
- **The Financial Times**:[19] *"Curricula are still not providing business graduates with commercial awareness."*

The criticisms don't end there. The experience of some large U.S. management consultants, traditionally a major hirer of business graduates,[20] is particularly edifying. Whilst they always also recruited non-business professionals such as lawyers, doctors, and philosophers, the proportion of non-MBAs they have been hiring has increased in recent years. In 2000, for example, the Boston Consulting Group hired 20% of its consultants without MBAs, Booz Allen and Hamilton planned to hire one third without graduate business degrees, and more than half of the consultants at McKinsey & Company did not have an MBA.[21]

All the new non-MBAs were given special training on three- or four-week programs to learn the basics of business. How did they fare? Internal studies[22] conducted by the firms found that the non-MBAs did no worse and, in some cases, better than their business school counterparts. The London office of the Boston Consulting Group, for example, reported that the *"non-MBAs were receiving better evaluations, on average, than their peers who had gone to business school,"* while a study at McKinsey of people on the job one, three, and seven years found that at all three points the people without MBAs were as successful as those with the degree. Another internal study[23] by an outside consulting firm also *"determined that the people... hired from high-end business schools were no better at integrative thinking than the undergraduates... hired from top-notch liberal arts programs."*

Illustrative of life on the business school campus are the commentaries of two graduate students attending Stanford's Graduate School: *"Learning is not an explicit goal"*[24] and *"the core curriculum taught at business schools is irrelevant, and that the utility of a business school degree is to provide a pedigree rather than learning."*[25] In fact business school curricula have changed little over time. Course materials have been upgraded and some class offerings have changed, but the 1960s product is still quite recognizable in the 1990s.[26] Little has changed since.

Another instructive volley that puts the whole problem into another cogent context surfaced in *The Observer* newspaper in 2002.[27] One of its senior commentators, Simon Caulkin, pointed out that in 2001 more undergraduates studied business and management—227,000 of them in fact—than any other subject. With the speciality accounting for 15% of university activity, he asked the no-nonsense question: *"Why is British management so bad?"* All those business graduates *"have not made the slightest dent in the U.K.'s persistent 20–30 per cent productivity shortfall compared with rival countries.*" Despite the runaway growth of business education, "*we still can't run a railway, telephone or a car company, or indeed any large-scale private enterprise outside oil and pharmaceuticals.*" He added, rather sadly: "*We are notably inept at rejuvenating our national institutions, the wrecks of which clutter the landscape like decaying hulks.*" And across the Atlantic a management education task force of the Association to Advance Collegiate Schools of Business concluded that the MBA curriculum and other business school courses were out of step with business needs.[28]

These reproaches, important in that they have endured through to the present day, have been repeated time and time again by the likes of Michael Porter and Lawrence McKibbin,[29] the Graduate Management Admissions Council[30] and Professors Mintzberg and Jonathan Gosling,[31] who noted that "*contemporary business education focuses on the functions of business more than the practice of managing.*"

In fact the disparagements of business teaching, including the MBA degree, go back 40 years, since when business schools have only partially addressed industry's preference for less theoretical instruction. In the United Kingdom, which has fashioned itself on the American model, the Owen Report into business schools voiced the tension between abstract and practical approaches to management.[32] A succession of other government and independent reports over the following two decades highlighted the continuing tug-of-war between practical and academic approaches, variously followed by initiatives such as the introduction of part-time or modular MBA programs and MBA courses for specific industries or organizations; the arrival of business instruction in hybrid institutions, such as polytechnics and colleges; and the imposed increase in levels of work experience prior to the commencement of the MBA.[33] What appears to have happened is that industry pressure for more *practice* in the curriculum was misinterpreted as a plea to raise entry qualifications and make existing business education more widely available. Few business schools saw it as direct criticism of the way in which they taught the business of business. Now, the advent of the flexible labor market has made the practical awareness of institutional-specific experience an even more necessary component of the educational mix, arguably, also, at pre-tertiary levels. This latter point is because most managers are not management trained. More often than not, the main criterion for their appointment is vocational competence, with the conventional rationalisation being: "If you're the best cook, you're the best choice to manage the kitchen."

Some of these criticisms suggest where broader educational black holes exist but what of the specific efforts made to accommodate experiential learning itself and associated decision making?

The nearest it gets to applying OM in any format that might be useful to combat the effects of the flexible labor market and poor decision making is through economic history, corporate history, business history, and case studies. This might seem all-embracing but, as tools to familiarize the next generation of workers with actual experience, *none* are widely used or *adequately* address the separate dysfunctional consequences of modern-day jobs churn or even its impact on decision making, in spite of long-standing censure.

There is also a portfolio of criticisms about traditional business education as they affect the issues that Experiential Learning proper would likely address.

The distinguished educator James Bailey, the Tucker Professor of Leadership at the School of Business, and Research Faculty at the Center for Learning, Graduate School of Education and Human Development, George Washington University, says: "*Business schools appeal to one another as scholarly communities through a plethora of academic journals that are utterly divorced from the challenges of everyday management.*"[34] They contend that although a scientific approach may be useful for the study of management, it is not clear that it helps in teaching management: "*The practice of management is best taught as a craft, rich in lessons derived from experience and oriented toward taking and responding to action.*" Elsewhere, Professor H. J. Leavitt notes: "*Business schools have been designed without practice fields.*"[35]

One further long-term criticism is the prevalent passive approach tutors use to impart information. This observation, key to the efficient application of experiential learning, is underscored by adult teaching specialist Dr. Stephen Brookfield's belief that teachers overlook the need for reflection.[36] His view is that students need "*interplay between action and reflection,*" proposing that curricula should not be studied in artificial isolation but rather that ideas, skills, and insights learned in a classroom should be tested and experienced in real life. Formal study is thus "*rein-forced by some appreciation of reality.*"

Henry Mintzberg, professor of management studies at McGill University, is a passionate believer in the importance of practical knowledge. His view[37] is that the MBA program claims to be creating managers when they're not. "*The MBA is really about business which would be fine except that people leave these programs thinking they've been trained to do management. I think every MBA should have a skull and crossbones stamped on their forehead and underneath should be written: 'not prepared to manage.'*"

His disenchantment with existing business instruction has led to his pioneering what has been dubbed the anti-MBA or "Real-Alternative MBA," whose acronym RAMBA has been described as a "*sort of feminine Rambo.*" With the help of the United Kingdom's Lancaster University's Jonathan Gosling, he launched his International Masters in Practising Management (IMPM) in 1996 to give more emphasis to encouraging managers to become more reflective. The approach concentrates on the complexity of real managerial and organisational problems rather than specialized knowledge in subjects such as marketing or finance, with students studying issues from within their organisations rather than general case studies. Alongside Lancaster, IMPM has been introduced at McGill University in Canada; INSEAD in France; the Indian Institute of Management in Bangalore, India; and with a group of academics from Hitotsubashi University, Kobe University; and the Advanced Institute of Science and Technology in Japan. In the IMPM, all students must be practicing managers and all must be sponsored by their companies, which include Alcan Aluminum Ltd., AstraZeneca PLC, Deutsche Lufthansa, the International Federation of the Red Cross and Red Crescent Societies, Matsushita Communication Industrial Co. Ltd., Motorola, and the Royal Bank of Canada. While these activities concentrate on experiential learning for employees, they do not address the loss of institutional knowledge if and when attendees join the flexible labor market.

Returning to business education's various proxies for experiential learning, economic history is the evolutionary study of fiscal practice as it affects national and international economies, a largely theoretical discipline that is unconnected with the intimate nature of running a real business. It addresses economic theory using econometric measuring techniques called cliometrics, a combination of mathematical economics and statistics. Its purpose is to provide economic interpretations of history, a la Adam Smith's 18th century theory about free trade which played an important part in the Industrial Revolution. Whilst providing a valuable macro perspective of how financial systems work, which may be practical for economists and important to academics, it is of only peripheral benefit for sharp-end businessmen and women having to deal with the micro issues of running a company or other type of organization. It is, for some inexplicable reason, seen as more valuable to managers than corporate and business history. Its use is, actually, in decline within business schools, with many departments being subsumed within non-business history units.[38]

Economic history is, of course, distinct from corporate history, which is the memoir of individual companies and other institutional bodies. As an educational medium, it is also widely ignored. Few business schools—or for that matter ordinary schools in more suitable formats—put them on their reading lists to provide their students with some sort of familiarity ahead of the intended industries in which they might want to work.

The nature of their creation (they are usually funded by the subject organizations) is one reason—in many cases they are deemed sycophantic, justifiably—but even those researched and written by academics and non-academic historians that are perceived as being credible, are ignored. Corporate histories are the most comprehensive and portable repositories of institutional memory and are even widely shunned as induction tools by the subject organizations themselves, their use seen as narrow-application celebratory mediums for important anniversaries.

The rationale is not entirely consistent. Client funding is common practice in many other areas of academic research, yet in this area of business, its use is institutionally shunned as a learning medium for students. In the United Kingdom at least, this is despite long-standing and credible endorsements of their potential value from luminaries such as Sir Arthur Knight, an early chairman of the textile company Courtaulds and a key figure behind the creation of the Manchester Business School in the 1960s. Corporate history, he believed, was as important to the education and training of businessmen as was the study of political history to future statesmen or military history to future generals.[39] And at the political level, Alex Fletcher, a former secretary of state for corporate and consumer affairs in Margaret Thatcher's Government, said:[40] *"There is a great deal of material in our schools and elsewhere about how babies are born but there is a tremendous shortage of publications about how businesses are born. Only a tiny number of people know there really was a Mr. Barclay, a Mr. Beecham, a Mr. Cadbury, a Mr. Rolls and a Mr. Royce, and the marvelous stories of how they created these now world-famous companies. Generations can only understand these examples if they learn and understand the process, innovation and the leadership that made it possible."*

An indicator of the perceived worth of those subject-funded corporate histories that *do* see the light of day can be judged by the internal audiences given to them, reflecting the organizations' perceived applications. In the United Kingdom the company's requirement for Bowater's 1981 history, for example, was 300 copies. Elsewhere Phoenix Assurance's order for the 1986 printing of the first volume of its history was 750. Each of the four volumes of the Hong Kong and Shanghai Banking Corporation's history, published from 1988 to 1991, received a company order for 1,600 copies; the majority was still in storage in 1997. Three thousand copies of Pilkington's 1977 history were still in storage piles 14 years later. Less heavyweight approaches received equally parsimonious audiences. When Blue Circle Industries published its corporate history in 1988, 7,000 copies ended up undistributed; while books were given to all directors free of charge, shareholders, current and previous employees and pensioners were offered them at a discounted price of £4.95. Just 100 employees and a few shareholders took up the offer. The book took four years to research and write by a Cambridge history graduate.

The approach by other countries is enlightening and certainly more attuned to a pre-designed application.[41] In Germany, BASF's 1990 history (*"so that employees would be able to identify the part they played within the company"*) had a print run of 313,000. Hoechst's 1988 biography (*"to imprint and reinforce an identity and loyalty across a group"*) circulated more than 170,000 copies plus. Bayer's 1988 history (*"there is a high awareness of history and tradition"*) was 185,000. With a budget of DM1m, Deutsche Bank's 1970 history got a 40,000 order, a purpose articulated by Hilmar Kopper, spokesman of the board of managing directors: *"The political and economic events which have taken place over the past 18 months* (he was referring to German reunification) *have, I believe, demonstrated that a knowledge of history is essential if we are to understand the problems of today. Understanding the present and looking towards the future mean that we need to analyse the past. Only by examining history closely can we establish the necessary distance between ourselves and the world today, and this enables us to see current problems in relative terms and form an independent opinion. I believe that being familiar with and understanding history can contribute substantially towards self-realisation and the establishment of identity, not only of an individual but also of an institution, In addition, it educates us in something which is of infinite importance to all of us—a sense of responsibility for the future."*

In the United States, the 1983 history of heavy engineering company Cooper Industries (*"to strengthen the group identity with acquired employees"*) had a print run of 75,000. The call for the 1987 biography of Abbott Laboratories was 50,000, Merck's 1991 history (as *"an employee motivator"*) 37,000, Eli Lilly's 1975 history (*"it's important to us"*) 30,000 and H.B. Fuller Company's 1987 book 24,000 copies. Of those that had an even more specific purpose, Cooper Industries used its 1983 history as a post-acquisition tool to primarily strengthen its group identity with all bought-in employees. *"We saw it primarily as an internal tool, to strengthen the identity of our employees with Cooper Industries by preserving and welding together in one book the histories of a large number of formerly independent companies that had been acquired over the years and were now product lines, operations or divisions of Cooper Industries,"* said T. W. Campbell, the company's vice president, public affairs.

For wider conceptual advocacy, London Business School's John Hunt confirms the genre's role as a means of fostering successful bonding. Pointing to religious organizations and the military as examples of institutions with well-planned history-orientated induction processes, Professor Hunt says: *"History can provide the stories, myths and legends for the new or merged culture."* Alluding directly to the 50% failure rate of acquisitions and mergers, his research[42] says there are compelling financial reasons for assisting in the integration process and transferring the acquired peoples' commitment to the firm's new owners—*"... winning the hearts and minds is an immediate necessity. Without their commitment it is difficult to achieve the operational and strategic objectives of the acquisition."* He points out that employees are at their most receptive at the time they are most inquisitive—immediately after an acquisition. Confirmation of corporate history's capacity to do this can be seen in the other examples of companies that have specifically used the genre as an induction tool. Proctor & Gamble, for example, which produced two corporate histories over four decades, is currently updating its biography expressly as an induction tool for new employees. In Japan, where many companies produce their corporate histories every 10 years, NEC, the electronics company, describes its latest history as a "*bible*" for new employees; the book, it says, provides a way "*to convey the company's culture of management and tradition to the next generation of employees.*"

In contrast to economic history and corporate history, business history is the more general historical study of the subject that builds a general appreciation of the contribution of single enterprises into the wider sector, industry, and national economic context. It is a field that is supposed to be sourced on individual corporate history. Only the United States has given the genre any serious attention, albeit in a small number of top universities. For example, Harvard is the only university where business history is a compulsory component of all first-year student teaching.

Once again, this is a subject, in the United Kingdom at least, that has had long-standing and credible support but little usage at student level. The late Sir Peter Parker, a former chairman of British Rail, said: "…. *business history is a missing dimension throughout the educational system. We need to build back into the business school approach the significance of a historical perspective.*"[43] It is no less an observation that one of the yardsticks for most other professions—for example music, architecture, art, soldiering, politics, and so on—is that their generic history is recognized as separate and discrete academic fields of learning. In most business curricula, both corporate history and wider business history is studiously avoided as a teaching tool.

The other device that is educationally designed to offer up institutional experience is case studies. They are almost always subject specific and, as such, disaggregate their inter-relationship with other management factors and influences. They often represent examples in other geographical areas. Dr. Bruce Lloyd, Professor of Strategic Management at South Bank University in London, is one academic who is critical of education's narrow preoccupation with this approach:[44] *"Despite the widespread acceptance of the concept of case studies, more needs to be done. What is now needed is to more closely integrate these ideas into the 'Learning Organisation' and 'Knowledge Management' developments. A Knowledge/Learning approach only makes any sense if we understand our history and put the insights that come from serious reflection on it, into more effective action than would otherwise be the case. Without this integration of past, present and future, there is little chance that the pressure for change in society today will end up by being anything remotely close to what we would all like to define as progress."*

Mintzberg and Lampel's position[45] is that teachers *"cannot replicate true managing in the classroom. The case study is a case in point: Students with little or no management experience are presented with 20 pages on a company they do not know and told to pronounce on its strategy the next day."* Elsewhere Bailey and Ford argue[46] that although a scientific approach may be useful for the study of management, it is not at all clear that it helps in teaching management. *"The practice of management is best taught as a craft, rich in lessons derived from experience and oriented toward taking and responding to action."*

At this point it is necessary to point up the obvious exception to this text's supposition that the flexible labor market impacts on productivity. It is the United States, which has the highest rates of both employee turnover and productivity, an outturn that would then contradict this author's model. The explanation, which endorses the country's wide liaison with a business legacy, its keenly shared social attentiveness to most things business and an ambitious migrant community whose learning is necessarily acute, also serves to underline why American managers are better experiential learners than the rest of the world. That said, Proudfoot's estimate[47] of the United States' 7.6% GDP cost of wasted productivity (see Table 1.1, Page 8) is still high enough to warrant further attention.

Uniquely, the United States has been formally providing successive generations with a business inheritance since the 1920s, when both corporate and business history were first and formally recognised as separate scholarly disciplines. Pioneered at Harvard Business School, where the well-known pre-occupation with the practical study of change is focused on putting business in its historical context, business history has been one of the most popular electives by business students for more than a decade at least and—as already indicated—is a compulsory component of all first-year teaching. At last count, there is a dedicated core community of around 400 academic business historians across the country. The subject is considered important enough to be a separate functional division of America's Academy of Management.

The value of providing an inheritance can be seen in the related science sector, which is the world's leader. The broader-based history of science was also acknowledged as an independent discipline in the 1920s. Alongside the enormous number of U.S.-produced books now available on the history of science, there are more than 60 American universities[48] offering dedicated higher degrees in the history of science, technology, and medicine. In addition, many colleges offer a concentration in history of science at the undergraduate level. More than 90 years after its importance was first recognised, the History of Science Society, which promotes United States teaching in the field, describes the subject as a bridging discipline that involves exposing students to more than the technical skills and theories of the natural sciences. Its view is that scientific literacy is a necessity in a culture pervaded by scientific values and crucially dependent on the applications of scientific knowledge—*"one that students, parents, educators, and political leaders in the U.S. all demand."*

It is also instructive to look at the Japanese experience. Historically, Japan's staff churn was low (in fact the industrialized world's lowest) with a productivity to rival the United States' and coincided with a keen interest in business history in the early 1970s when, on the instructions of the then crown prince, a business historian was appointed to every faculty of business and commerce in the country. Today, Japan's core community of business historians equals the numbers in the United States. Since the early 1990s, however, Japan's employee turnover rose in tandem with its recession, albeit not as fast as employee turnover in prior recessions in Western countries. Nevertheless, Japan's productivity has fallen away to the point where it now ranks just below the United Kingdom's, with the possible part-explanation of its woes including that it is not as good at Experiential Learning as previously.

Business education's myopia also extends to the important subject of decision making proper. In spite of it being the single most important skill of any manager, it is not taught as a *dedicated* subject in most curricula. It is as if one is educated in general subjects such as marketing, finance, and so on, and then it is assumed that how to make good decisions will follow by default.

This apparent inattention to an important discipline disguises a bewildering clutch of widely unused and mainly academically devised theoretical approaches to the subject that are available and categorized under the broad-based classification of Decision Analysis. They include techniques such as Analytic Hierarchy Process (AHP), Bayesian Updating, Outranking, Subjective Judgment Theory, Utility Assessment, Matrix, Cost—Benefit Analysis, and the Decision Tree—the last three being the most commonly known. Matrix, for example, utilizes a subjective weight assignment for alternative criteria, its main drawback being that it cannot account for interdependence between so-called best alternatives. Cost–benefit analysis, which provides a quantitative format for reckoning the range of benefits and costs surrounding a prospective decision, aggregates the effects over time using an approach called discounting, and arriving at a "present value" or "payback period." In its simplest form, it is carried out using only monetary costs and benefits, but a more sophisticated approach tries to put a financial value on intangible costs and benefits, which makes the calculation highly subjective. Other criticisms include the imprecise techniques used to measure diverse benefits and costs and the fact that, to some, environmental concerns fall properly under the realm of ethics rather than economics.

The Decision Tree is an abstract methodology in which alternative decisions and their implications can be evaluated via a genealogy-type visual aid. Its main criticisms include overfitting—when the tree matches random variations of the target values in the training data that are not replicated in other samples. Its other shortcoming is its instability, when the tree fits the data well, predicts well, and conveys a good story, but then, if some of the original data is replaced with a fresh sample and a new tree is created, a completely different root-and-branch picture may emerge using completely different inputs in the splitting rules and, consequently, conveying a completely different story. However, as loyal as followers of any of these techniques might be, the historical shortcomings of industry and commerce confirm that good decision making is a far more practical discipline than these methodologies accommodate. This author would suggest that their usage is rare—and corresponding managers' performance hardly impressive.

A research paper by the management consultancy Capgemini[49] found that the most effective individual decision-making styles reveal a strong preference for qualities that support a collaborative decision making approach while the ability to "make a call" quickly and stick by a decision, determination to seek out the best possible solution and willingness to take risks are the least popular characteristics. Managers, the study found, depend on external advice in more than 50% of critical decisions. In fact, central government in the United Kingdom uses management consultants and other "advisers" to help its managers push through public sector reforms. According to the analysis[50] of a national newspaper, the cost of proxying its own managerial skills is a staggering £1.75 billion a year. This excludes the money that local councils, NHS trusts and other public bodies spent on consultants outside Whitehall. However, these figures are presented, they are hardly an advertisement for the decision making skills of many managers, whose determinations are often the rubber-stampings of others'.

That managerial skills are less than optimal even comes straight from the horse's mouth—managers themselves.[51] Their own assessment—in this case by senior British managers or direct board report positions in companies turning over more than £200 million a year—is that an astonishing one in four of their decisions is wrong. According to the same Capgemini study, the rate in the financial services sector is even higher—nearly one in three. With an average 20 "business critical" decisions taken by each manager every year, the financial impact of which is computed to be worth an average £3.4 million each, this equates to a wrong determination every eight weeks by each of every one of an average 33 decision-makers in every organization.

Wider performance figures come from a study[52] published in Harvard Business Review that found that 55% of leaders are associated with below-average corporate performance. Just 15% of the individuals studied over 25 years—the period of growing business education—showed a consistent ability to manage innovation and organizational change. And, for an anecdotally overwhelming indicator of the extent of ineffectual decision making, an entry of "poor management" into an Internet search engine[53] found 73 million references worldwide, massively a third of the number for the most popular word, "sex," on the same search engine.

These "snapshots" should not detract from the fact that the majority of decisions that managers make are right, otherwise a lot more institutions would not survive. But the same general performance would likely not be tolerated among their vocational subordinates.

In truth, learning itself has its own clutch of associated methodologies. The list—there are at least 35 of them and worth recording—is significant for their breadth of choice, among them authentic learning; accelerating learning; adaptive learning; anticipatory learning; appreciative learning; celleration learning; cognitive learning; collaborative learning; competency-based learning; competitive learning; concurrent learning; constant learning; cooperative learning; creative learning; single-, double-, and triple-loop learning; high-impact learning; interorganizational learning; interpartner learning; innovative learning; leading learning; mechanistic learning; organizational learning; outcome-based learning; parenthetic learning; programed learning; self-directed learning; rote learning; situated learning; strategic learning; total quality learning; transformational learning; virtual learning; and virtuous learning.

Some are highly relevant and have similarities to David Kolb's reflective approach but, once again, do not allow anything other than the usage of current practice of replaced employees. The rest are mostly obscure, the creation of inventive individuals, suggesting that the universal process of learning has become so fragmented into specialized branches that the practice has become disaggregated. The implication for generalists, such as managers, is that attention is drawn away from understanding the universal principles of learning and, in the case of business, of decision making. People have become so used to simply having data and information given to them that they have become unskilled at creating knowledge for themselves or their employers. Learning, and particularly the inter-related way of decision making, has gone astray, with its specializations paradoxically inhibiting one's own organic development—much like the plethora of sophisticated toys now available to children, whose ability to play inventively has subsequently been degraded. If anything, academics' and managers' surplus of choice signifies the importance given to the process of acquiring knowledge, but their widespread neglect must also suggest a pervasive corporate confusion about which to use or their perceived ineffectiveness.

The above reproaches are perplexing in a relatively advanced world but raise the spectre of how much better—and specifically cheaper and better value for consumers—things could have been if the education system was not so resistant to these critical bystanders. It all becomes a little more understandable when set against Robert Hayes's already-mentioned observation[54] (see Chapter 1, Page 9) that the achievements are *despite* management's best efforts and his—and this author's and others'— appraisal that managers do not learn easily from the example of precedent.

As the critics say—and what the evidence shouts for—are more *functional* managers, not just vocationally-orientated individuals but those who have been managerially-trained to make good and better decisions. In truth, there is an elemental difference in their way their skills are derived. To re-emphasise Chapter 1's point (Page 7) about the difference between the educational input of blue-collar and white-collar workers, the teaching of the former is basically instruction received while the teaching of the latter is instruction acquired out of an abstracted process of critical reflection of prior experience, the ability to reflect constructively and, finally, to conclude appropriately. It is not something the vocationally orientated or even the managerially trained are able to do in today's walkabout jobs market.

The opportunity value for academia is that individuals need to be taught *how to learn* from actual experience. Such is the importance of experiential learning in today's workplace of 'here today and gone tomorrow', which **none** of the conventional learning tools address.

Now for all those experiential **non**-learners!

CHAPTER 5

"I Forgot to Remember!"

Experience. The wisdom that enables us to recognize in an undesirable old acquaintance the folly that we have already embraced.
—Ambrose Bierce, U.S. author[1]

The record of how well and/or how quickly industry and commerce learns from experience is not good.

From Jean Piaget's Einstein-applauded observations of how children learn to Professor David Kolb's reflective process to transform knowledge into new knowledge has taken more than 80 years. Kolb's own efforts have been around for a quarter of a century, with his weary statement that his Experiential Learning theory only started to be recognized empirically after more than 10 years. And alongside everybody else's considerable efforts, some of which have been related in Chapter 4, there is still little respite from productivity growth's heavy hand (see Figure 2.1, Page 12), confirming that whatever strategies are being used, decision makers continue to endorse the observation that Roger Hayes found in the 1843 edition of the *Edinburgh Review* that managers don't learn well from experience.[2]

To put perspective on this statement within the broad compass of the impressive record of success in many economies, there is an unnecessarily high incidence of recurring failure that, if decision making were only more rigorously applied, could be viewed as delayed success. Given the enormous cost of failure and waste that could be avoided, the potential for productivity gains would be substantial, as would be the organizations' automatic advantage with pushy competitors.

For a striking illustration of the scale of the whole subject's neglect, one need only defer to *The Times of London*, one of whose reporters had discerned the high incidence of continuing failure in the public sector, which, in many countries, is now the biggest of employers. He did a computer search in Hansard, the official record of all legislative utterances in the Westminster Parliament, for the words "no stone unturned," which he decoded was "*an inflated way to claim energetic action*" for something gone wrong.[3] Staggeringly, his computer came up with the number 4,933 over the 14-year period to 2002. "*Is it really possible that someone in the House of Lords, the Commons or elsewhere in the political machine has declared their intention to leave no stone unturned, on average, once every single day for the past 14 years?*" he wrote. This book's author's own Google search in July 2008, when the first edition of this manuscript was being written, was even more surprising. The words "*not fit for purpose*," a more fashionable description of management dysfunction first used in 2006 when a U.K. Government minister, John Reid, acknowledged the leadership and management deficiencies at the Home Office, yielded 132,000 references for the whole economy—180 times more than *The Times* figure. How many of these citations were entirely new or repeated mistakes was not counted, but the list of reinvented wheels and other unlearned lessons—also a function of experiential *non*-learning—is long, both in the public and private sectors in the United Kingdom Collectively, the figure for similar dysfunction elsewhere in the world must be astronomical, as already suggested by Proudfoot Consulting's estimate of wasted productivity across some OECD countries (see Table 1.1, Page 8).[4]

The example of *The Times*' Hansard search is instructive if one looks a bit closer at the U.K. Government's business. Today—2011–2012—the Government's "sales," its tax revenues, are around £575 billion,[5] with around 6 million people in its employment. The contemporary example, below, flags up the problems that happen to be self-recognized, as are the potential domino effects and the lamest-ever solution for the public equivalent of a Chief Executive Officer. For years, politicians and civil servants have felt themselves exempt from the rigors of rudimentary economics to provide value for the same unit of currency that provides its revenue.

Before the 2010 British general election, Alistair Darling, the last Chancellor of the Exchequer, was interviewed by the BBC for a high-profile series outlining the activities of "The Great Offices of State."[6] Referring to the period in office of Gordon Brown, the programme's presenter, Michael Cockerall, made the observation that staff turnover during his predecessor's time in office was high and that the average age of employees was significantly lower than previous periods.

Mr Darling's response illustrated precisely the difficulty in just one U.K. Government department. "*When I came back here as Chancellor, Nick Macpherson, the Permanent Secretary [2005-], said to me: 'Do you know that there are only three people here [in the Treasury] who have ever been through a recession'. He [Mr Macpherson] was at the time worried …. that the collective memory of the institution was beginning to fade and I think there is another lesson there …. there is something to be said for ensuring that you've got sufficient people who can remember the nuts and bolts of how the economy works, who know what to do in a crisis, who know how to respond. I'm not making a case for the place being full of Victor Meldrews* [fictional character, British sitcom 'One foot in the grave' featuring irascible pensioner]. *What I'm saying is that you do have to have some mechanism ensuring that you remember things. You remember that things can go wrong as right. When they go wrong you remember how to fix them.*"

Mr Darling's loosely identified call for "*some mechanism*" to be embedded in institutions is instructive for its formless character but this was still not as unimaginative—and professionally embarrassing—as would be the later solution attempted by the departmental administrators of his successor, George Osborne.

Less than two years after Mr Darling made his "*some mechanism*" suggestion came confirmation that the problem was even more widespread across Government.[7] According to the respected think tank, the Institute for Government, turnover of top staff risked leaving the civil service short of expertise, with the Institute's Programme Director, Jill Rutter, warning that such high levels of turnover could have long-term consequences.

Specifically, the Government was dealing with an unprecedented churn of senior civil servants with a majority of ministers in posts for longer periods than their permanent secretaries. Staff turnover rates in some departments were as high as 30%, a rate of disruption that had surpassed the traditionally more volatile private sector.

The situation, the Institute disclosed, was particularly acute at the very top of the civil service and within Downing Street, with an extraordinary turnover of officials over the previous 16 months. The institute warned that, at a time when the Government was attempting to make significant public-sector savings, the loss of institutional knowledge could adversely affect the running of departments.

The extent of the problem was highlighted by the en masse departure of the Permanent Secretary and three director generals in the Department for Education, their jobs being filled by people "acting up." Elsewhere, the longest-serving member of the top team at the Department for Communities and Local Government had joined the board just before the election; everyone else had been there less time than the ministers. Alongside this, the Prime Minister's top Foreign Affairs team had changed completely, with the appointment of two National Security advisers since the election. Broader turnover in the Foreign Office had increased by 8.1% over the previous year. A new EU and Global Affairs adviser and a permanent replacement for the chair of the Joint Intelligence Committee had yet to be announced.

And in Mr Darling's former department, the Treasury, the exodus of personnel had continued, with staff turnover rising from 22% in 2010 to 28% in 2011. This included six Director and Director General level officials, among them the Director General of Public Services, the Head of Budget Planning and the Director of International Finance. *The Independent* newspaper reported that two Departmental officials had remarked that the Treasury's turnover was *"higher than McDonald's."*[8]

Other problem areas were in the Department for Culture, Media and Sport, where staff churn had increased by 10.5% over the year. The Department of Health was undergoing a complete restructuring of its top team, with three new Director General jobs out for open competition, while the Department for the Environment was about to reorganise at Director General and Director level. The Department for Environment, Food and Rural Affairs was about to reorganise its top structure at Director General and Director level. In the Department for Education, the Permanent Secretary and three Director General roles were being filled by people "acting up" since the top team had departed en masse, while work on "open public services" in The Cabinet Office had been the responsibility of four different Deputy Directors since the 2010 election. Also, the Government was already on its third Chief Information Officer.

With the Institute warning that the turmoil in the Civil Service was not yet over, George Osborn's Treasury officials decided to grapple with the exodus in their own eccentric way. Their lame solution was to send out emails to remaining staff asking whether they had any friends interested in applying for unfilled jobs.

It is instructive that departmental administrators saw the problem as little more than a replacement exercise; no one saw the domino outcome that even if replacements *were* found, there was still no solution to the problem of their predecessor's disappeared prior knowledge and wisdom.

It has been left to a maverick politician to spot one of the darker underlying reasons for government's poor decision making skills that also resonates with the flexible labor market. She believes there is a deliberate policy by some civil servants who want to obstruct policy, an echo of the successful satirical British sitcom *Yes, Minister* and *Yes, Prime Minister* that was widely recognized as art imitating life. Margaret Hodge, MP, the latest Chair of the Public Accounts Committee (PAC), a body that oversees government expenditure, explains in terms that echoes the customary short job tenure of the political classes, what she described as the "*inconsistency of leadership*": "*How do you move up the ladder in the civil service? Well, you do it by doing two years in a job and then switching. And that is just crazy because you end up never taking responsibility for a project from beginning to end. You're never accountable.*" There is a "*lack of real clarity about who is responsible.*"[9]

Ms Hodge spotted what was happening when she was leader of London's Islington Council for 10 years before being elected an MP and holding three ministerial jobs under the Labour Government. Her belief is that the business of Government has become too complicated for transient ministers to fully hold their civil service officials to account. "*Trying to get a policy changed if the officials did not agree with you was well-nigh impossible. Submissions would come up late. They would then come in a way which you didn't want. Sometimes the policy option you wanted wouldn't even be there so you'd have to go back and make them write it again. There was playing for delay because they knew you were transient. And that's one of the really important things—the political class is much more transient than the administrative class.*"

In her new role Hodge is determined to change things by attempting to rip up decades of constitutional convention and hold civil servants accountable for their decisions—even if they have moved on. She also wants to extend the remit of the PAC to include companies contracted by the Government to do the State's work. "*We need to rethink where ministerial accountability stops and civil service accountability starts. These are really difficult issues and there are clearly tensions in redefining these accountabilities but just because it's difficult it should not become an excuse for not tackling it. It's an issue that needs to be tackled because its time has come.*"

Now, a more transient Civil Service is complicating the problem even further with Organizational Memory (OM) disappearing rather than being domestically swept under departmental carpets. If civil service culture does eventually change, Ms Hodge might well solve the problem of accountability but there is still the issue of the departmental knowledge, experience and institutional wisdom regularly walking out of the front door rather than just deploying elsewhere in the Civil Service.

With Number 10 Downing Street's particular turmoil in mind, this point's knock-on effect was articulated by one of Conservative Party's elder statesmen, Lord Tebbit, who served in Mrs Thatcher's cabinet for six years, and latterly as Chairman of the party. In a particularly criticised period of Prime Minister David Cameron's premiership, Lord Tebbit accused Number 10 of relying too much on advisers who lacked "*experience or much understanding of the party or politics.*"[10]

It is not that Government has not been trying to solve its productivity shortfalls. There have been dozens of reports flagging up the problem as well as the professed fixes over the years. And the interesting thing in many of them, the words used to explain the problem and the solution are exactly the language that runs through this manuscript. Even before the current credit crunch started to bite in earnest, the National Audit Office, which scrutinises public spending on behalf of Parliament, attributed Government waste to departments' failure to learn from rapid staff turnover, day-to-day mistakes, "*ineffective mechanisms*" to support learning and the need to "*institutionalise the systematic reflection on performance after projects.*"[11]

The MP who chaired the Commons Public Accounts Committee at the time, Edward Leigh, articulated the official written word: it was *"obvious that government needs to get better at learning lessons from past mistakes. Before embarking on projects, departments should identify lessons from what has gone well or badly in the past. And they need to examine what has worked well for other organisations."* Fed up with investigating failures caused by the mistakes time after time, he said that departments had to understand that the best time to learn how to improve service delivery wasn't necessarily after a crisis or large-scale project, but *"day in, day out."*

To prove that all this is not new—and that much experiential non-learning is still taking place after many years—there is a catalogue of historical examples of poor decision making that shows up the quality of administrators and their determinations.

Over budget and overdue were (and still are) characteristics in many U.K. public projects such as the Channel Tunnel and its rail link, the British Library, the Concorde, the Limehouse Link road tunnel, the Cardiff Bay Barrage, the Luton Airport extension, the Welsh Assembly, and the Scottish Parliament—the latter ending up at 11 times its original budget (£391 million) and 3 years overdue. The experience of several of London Transport's projects over the 10-year period to 2000 is particularly striking. Against the background of managers' insistence of long-time underfunding on the London Underground, the National Audit Office's (NAO) conclusion that much of the £10 billion investment on the Jubilee Line Extension, the Docklands Light Railway, and the wider tube system—equivalent to more than 10% of the entire public sector investment during the period—was wasted because of a failure to integrate systems effectively. Where the story gets even more sobering is the conclusion by the NAO that these performance failures would recur in future investment projects *"because learning from one project was not easily transferred to the next."*[12]

There have been continuous safety and punctuality issues on the railways under both public and private ownership. Unable to improve its timetable sufficiently, the country's largest railway defaulter, Thameslink, simply moved the goalposts by increasing the journey times of its trains in peak periods when the company was liable for the highest fines.[13] These penalties cost it £2.2 million in 2002.

At the turn of the year 2000, 10 of the 27 *planned* millennial landmarks were similarly overdue or over budget, or both. Overall in the public sector in 2001 the NAO found that slightly less than 75% of building projects were either over budget or overdue.

As if to confirm the United Kingdom's inability to learn from its own experiences, the BAA (previously the British Airports Authority) did a market test to compare building costs in another country where labor and material costs were similar to those in Britain.[14] U.S. contractors were asked to tender for an office block identical to a development already underway at Heathrow for British Airways. Built to U.S. designs and specifications, the American building came out 32% cheaper, thanks to the U.S. architects and engineers spending less time "*reinventing*" wheels.

Over in farming, the non-learning problem is also endemic. Bovine Spongiform Encephalopathy (BSE), eggs, chickens, variant Creutzfeldt-Jakob disease (vCJD), salmonella, *E. coli*, and foot-and-mouth disease have cost the nation dearly—the latter putting in a bill estimated in excess of £9 billion last time round.[15]

The foot-and-mouth and BSE debacles are especially notable. In the case of foot-and-mouth disease, the 2001 outbreak followed similar outbreaks in 1952 and 1967. Post-event audits at the time published clear lessons that had to be learned, evidently in vain. Following the 1988 BSE disaster, which also yielded an official list of lessons to be learned from cannibalistic recycling, officials from the Ministry of Agriculture admitted in 2000 that feed containing cows' blood products, tallow, and gelatine was *still* being fed to cows and other livestock, including newborn calves as a cheap feed to replace their mothers' milk.

Of the overall extra £1 trillion spent by the government between 1997 and 2007, "*there is precious little to show for it*," according to management consultant David Craig's book on how so much money has been wasted.[16]

In the United States, the Ford Motor Company illustrates the effects of one of corporate amnesia's causes—the flexible labor market—in the production of its Taurus model car.[17] The previous version of the car had been a big hit because it met the needs of big-car buyers better than most of its rivals. It then experienced a loss of its so-called design memory when it massively cut back on jobs in the recession of the early 1990s. As a result, the new model was largely reengineered from scratch. Having forgotten what its customers wanted, the result was a model that failed to capture the buyers' imagination.

The price of forgetting—specifically how often dominant companies complacently ignore the effects of mature markets and new technologies—is illustrated at IBM, another of the United States' more successful companies.[18] In the 1980s a smug Remington yielded dominance of the typewriter market to the electronic age—and to IBM. Almost immediately IBM made the same expensive mistake by reacting inappropriately to a technology that threatened its own core business. On the surface it simply misjudged one of its product's life cycles; but in reality, it mishandled the emergence of personal computers, vastly underrating the impact that they would have on its larger mini and mainframe businesses. A better memory of how Remington reacted to similar conditions might have encouraged IBM to give its originally independent PC unit a longer life and avoided the United States' biggest annual corporate loss of $4.9 billion in 1992. In fact, a slightly longer sighted memory may have helped IBM to avoid the crisis in the first place. Before the computer age really took off, IBM always perceived itself as a service organization that provided information technologies to large companies. It is arguable that the company's problems occurred when it began to believe that it was a computer company. It regained profitability when it returned to its first principles and finally departed barely profitable PC making in 2004 when it sold out to Lenovo, China's leading PC maker, for $1.75 billion, catapulting the Chinese company into third place in the world's PC market.

For a while Apple Inc., which built itself on a culture that challenged employees to build cutting edge and affordable computers with a distinctive look, also lost its OM as it ran through four chief executive officers in as many years.[19] It subsequently successfully resurrected the past with iMac by reminding the public of the ground breaking Apple II and Macintosh when the company's founder, Steve Jobs, returned to lead the company. In effect, Jobs served as the organization's memory.

A persistent mistake is also evident in the way Citicorp regularly changes its regional organizational structure.[20] In recent years it has alternated between combining sales and operations, and keeping them separate. When they realize that sales was not getting the attention it needed in the highly competitive financial services industry, they separated them once again. The waste of resources has been colossal, as has its fall from grace.

Elsewhere, there is a large insurance group that is a good example of a similar case of forgetting as a result of downsizing.[21] Having slimmed its claims department, it found it was settling big claims too swiftly and too generously. It discovered it had laid off several long-term employees who had created an informal, but highly effective, way to screen claims. It subsequently reinstated them.

A U.S. service company experienced an organizational breakdown after a high level of turnover among frontline employees.[22] The potential revenue at a pharmaceuticals company was jeopardized for the next decade by experience shortfalls in departments across the organization's entire drug development cycle.[23] A senior financial consultant who resigned on a Friday night without notice put at risk 1,000 client relationships with $175 million of assets under management. And a high-tech company had to offer a $1 million project completion bonus to a key engineer to prevent delay in a new product launch after a high level of departmental departures.[24]

The finance sector is especially rich in examples of experiential *non-learning*, in particular banking, where the record of failures has left a decent trail of evidence that successive generations of highly paid bankers continually forget. A graphic example, which illustrates both the magnitude of the phenomenon and its pervasive nature, can be seen in the banking crisis of the 1980s and 1990s. In the early 1980s the U.K. banking community was badly mauled by bad debts in South America. Less than 10 years later it was again overwhelmed—this time from loan defaults elsewhere in the developing world. Speaking in 1991, the head of one of the United Kingdom's largest banks admitted that there were plenty of historical precedents on Latin American lending that "*should have put the red light up for everyone.*"[25] He added, "*We have got to ensure that the lessons of the recent past are not forgotten by the rising generation of bankers.*" As he was talking the banks were once again making similar errors of judgement—this time at home in the United Kingdom—with High Street lenders having to chalk up further provisions collectively totalling almost £4 billion in their 1992 accounts. This prompted one analyst to comment that "*the biggest worry is that banks do not seem to be capable of learning from their mistakes,*" a warning echoed in 1994 by a banking industry think tank that analyzed the massive write-offs. For the current sub-prime and credit crunch problems, the official lessons to be learned are still being assessed, but the odds are that the echo will be equally deafening.

Another example of how easily (and often) the opportunity to learn from experience is overlooked can be seen in the aftermath of the Barings bank collapse in the United Kingdom, when rogue trader Nick Leeson ran up £791 million of hidden losses while working for the company in Singapore. Less than a decade later, four traders at National Australia Bank lost AU$252 million (£100 million) in unauthorized foreign exchange trades. In 2002 another trader at Allied Irish bank managed to hide almost £700 million of investment losses before being found out. And more recently, an independent review at the petroleum company Royal Dutch Shell found that company executives knowingly hid a massive shortfall in oil and gas reserves. Management and infrastructure flaws continue to allow such events to persist. The lessons of Barings had clearly not been learned, and with expensive consequences. JP Morgan's £2 billion-plus derivative trading loss could be the latest of repeated scandals for the banking sector to admit to.

Ironically, at the time of the Shell scandal the company was consciously leveraging the concept of the Peter Senge-initiated The Learning Organization, a discipline that overlaps with Experiential Learning through building personal mastery and shared vision. Faced with dramatic changes and unpredictability in the world oil markets in the 1980s, Shell's planners had concluded that they no longer saw their task as producing a documented view of the future business environment five or 10 years ahead.[26] Instead, they re-conceptualized their basic task as fostering learning rather than devising plans and engaging managers to ferret out the implications of possible scenarios. By institutionalizing the learning process, they conditioned the managers—or so they thought—to be mentally prepared for the uncertainties in the business environment.

It is instructive to look at the learning example of BP, which, with the latest Deepwater Horizon disaster, has the worst safety track record of any major oil company operating in the United States. According to the Congress-created Occupational Safety and Health Administration (OSHA),[27] BP ran up more than 750 safety violations in the six-year period to 2010. On its own the repeated mistakes shows a deeply-ingrained inability to learn from its own experience but they also flag up how difficult it is for highly skilled employees to learn. The big puzzle is that BP already had a devoted Experiential Learning process in place called Learning Histories (see Chapter 3, Page 32).

The company's vulnerability record included:

- September 2004—Accident at BP's Texas City refinery kills two workers and injures a third. BP fined $109,500 for safety violations. Almost a year earlier a series of explosions rocked the refinery, with no reported loss of life.
- March 2005—Blast at the Texas City refinery kills 15 workers and injures more than 170. BP fined $21.3m for safety violations.
- July 2005—Thunder Horse offshore platform nearly sinks in wake of Hurricane Dennis in the Gulf of Mexico.
- March 2006—Oil spill in Alaska. Rupture in 34-in pipe leads to largest oil spill ever on the North Slope over two acres of snow-covered tundra.
- October 2009—Federal Occupational Safety Administration proposes to fine BP a record $87.4m for 709 new safety violations at its Texas City refinery.
- March 2010—OSHA fines BP $3m for 62 safety violations at Ohio refinery.
- April 2010—Deepwater Horizon drilling rig explodes, killing 11 workers and sending millions of gallons of oil gushing from BP's Macondo well. Estimates vary of the cost, a conservative one being $41.3 billion in clean up, compensation and other payouts in addition to the indirect adverse economic effects of reputational damage and lost customer confidence.[28]

The sequence is noteworthy for the similarity of problems and their concentrated timeline. Explosion, explosion, pipe rupture, pipe rupture, explosion and pipe rupture ..... The 2005 Thunder Horse accident, involving a backwardly installed valve and a shoddy pipeline weld in the wake of Hurricane Dennis, could, arguably, have been the precursor to Deepwater Horizon. "*It could have been catastrophic,*" according to Gordon A. Aaker Jr., a senior engineering consultant on the project.

"You would have lost a lot of oil a mile down before you would have even known. It could have been a helluva spill—much like the Deepwater Horizon."[29]

For BP, the big question is why did it become such big experiential non-learners over this period, way beyond any of its competitors? And, of course, whether this will continue? Quoting BP's own Steve Arendt, a safety specialist who assisted the company-appointed panel to investigate the company's refineries after the deadly 2005 explosion at its Texas City facility, that the company was *"very arrogant and proud and in denial,"* the conclusion of the New York Times[30] is that BP is *"chronically unable or unwilling to learn from its mistakes."*

While it is not known if Learning Histories were employed at Texas City, Thunder Horse or Deepwater Horizon so, then, what was the possible reason for the methodology not working at BP's Ohio refinery, where the company was fined for 62 safety violations in 2010?

Aside from "denial" and "arrogance," there are the obvious candidates of poor skills recruitment, decision-makers ignoring their existing learning processes and/or that the existing learning processes are less than rigorous. These aside, there is at least one other possible reason interrelated with the flexible labor market. Back in 2000, BP in the United States did not appear to be particularly concerned at the level of its employee churn and—presumably because the actual figures did not appear to be particularly high—did not publish any such statistics. In fact, the annual turnover rate for all industry sectors in the United States was at record-breaking levels at the time; before seasonal adjustment the average staff turnover across U.S. industry and commerce was an average 39.6% during the period 2001–2006,[31] meaning that average employer tenure was *less* than three years. By 2006, the year of the Alaska oil spill, a report in Fortune magazine was quoting a BP employee who had also worked at Texas City as saying there was *"constant staff turnover"* as new bosses would seek to beat the previous manager's performance numbers.[32] In 2008, BP was warning that recruiting people with experience had become a major challenge for the energy industry worldwide.[33] Then, non-retail corporate staff turnover was 11% (up from 9% the year earlier), a rate the company considered to be *"sustainable."* For 2011, chairman Carl-Henric Svanberg was recording in his 2012 Report and Accounts[34] that non-retail employee turnover for each of the previous three years was 15%, a level that was, presumably, approaching or was at *unsustainable* levels.

Factoring in the understanding that workplace discontinuity is the poorer teacher of lessons learned, consider the following causal scenario that tracks the awareness—or rather the unfamiliarity—of BP employees' company-specific experience since the year 2000. On the basis of recent workplace churn and an annual staff turnover indicative of an average seven-year tenure over the decade ending 2010—incidentally better than the average for most other businesses and organizations—BP would have wholly replaced a large majority of its total workforce by the 2006 date of the Alaska oil spill. By 2010, the date of Deepwater Horizon, *all* of the year 2000 employees would have moved on. As such, with so much second-hand awareness on site, the ability to benefit from its own experience will have been much reduced.

Run the same level of staff turnover forward from 2010 and the computation will show that **nobody** within BP will have any first-hand memory of Deepwater Horizon by 2017, thus also increasing the chances of more repeated incidents down the line.

But given the trillions of dollars squandered, the mother and father of experiential non-learning must belong to two other unlearned lessons, the first very modern, the second now more than six decades old. Both are of similar distinction and size and display a cyclonic degree of experiential non-learning. The combined costs of both are more than big enough to illustrate the importance of Experiential Learning's prime role of not having to relearn things again and again and yet again.

The first is the current credit crunch and its worldwide domino effects. Rhetorical the question might be but what value would former U.S. President George W. Bush, British Prime Minister Gordon Brown, and the other country leaders place on knowing how to solve the credit crisis or even knowing how they might have avoided the problem in the first place?

The reactions of almost everyone to this most serious of globalized threats to international prosperities since the 1930s were characterized by unnecessary delay—years in fact—in both acknowledging the problems and doing something about it, intervals that undoubtedly exacerbated the eventual crisis to its current proportions. In the United

States, where the problem originated, dogma was a further aggravating factor, demonstrating as clearly as it ever could the triumph of gospel—in this case, political gospel—over education. While everyone dithered, the arch-capitalist thought the perceived solution was too socialist, in spite of the fact that nationalization—the public ownership of private assets—had been used by them on numerous occasions over the past 150 years, even recently. Barring the unlikely scenario that the build-up was observed but consciously overlooked, the fact that the events even *occurred* in their magnitude show that they and their supposedly qualified advisers were unsuspecting, unprepared, or unqualified for what followed.

The "experiential learning" events from which lessons could have been learned to prevent the current credit crisis are numerous. All with elements that bear a resemblance to the events of 2008, they include:

- How overinflated booms invariably crash, including the Japanese property boom of the late 1980s and the 1990s dot-com collapse. In the case of the latter, shares of Internet companies soared, despite few of the firms actually making a profit. The crash had wider repercussions, with business investment falling and economies slowing.
- The mismanagement of long-term capital, specifically the 1998 collapse of the long-term capital management (LTCM). When Russia defaulted on its government bonds, investors fled to U.S. Treasury bonds and interest rate differences between bonds increased sharply. LTCM, which had borrowed heavily, stood to lose billions of dollars. In order to liquidate its positions, it would have to sell Treasury bonds, plunging the U.S. credit markets into turmoil and forcing up interest rates. The Fed, the central bank of the United States, persuaded many of the leading U.S. banks to bail out LTCM, which—after stability returned—was liquidated in 2000.
- How financial deregulation is not always beneficial. The 1985 U.S. Savings and Loans scandal, which followed financial deregulation in the 1980s, allowed savings institutions that were similar to British building societies to engage in more complex, and often unwise, financial transactions, in

order to compete with the big commercial banks. By 1985, many of these institutions were all but bankrupt, and a run began on S&L institutions in Ohio and Maryland. The U.S. government had insured many of the individual deposits in the S&Ls. It set up the Resolution Trust Company to take over and sell any S&L assets that it could, including repossessed homes.

Among the more numerous events from which solutions could have been learned much earlier are:

- The 1866 failure of a major London bank, which led to a key change in the role of central banks in managing financial crises. Overend and Gurney was a discount bank that provided money for commercial and retail banks in London, the world's financial center. When it declared bankruptcy in May 1866, many smaller banks were unable to get funds and went under, even though they were otherwise solvent. The Bank of England was given a new role as "the lender of last resort" to provide liquidity to the financial system during crises, in order to prevent a failure of one bank spilling over and affecting all the others. The new doctrine was implemented in the Barings Crisis in 1890, when losses made on its investments in Argentina were covered by the Bank of England to prevent a systemic collapse of U.K. banking. Secret negotiations by the Bank and London financiers led to the creation of an £18m rescue fund in November 1890, before the extent of Barings' losses became publicly known.
- The 1917 seizure in the United States of the railways to ensure the smooth transportation of goods, armaments, and troops during WWI. After the war ended, bondholders and stockholders were compensated and railways were returned to private ownership in 1920.
- The 1932 investments made by the Reconstruction Finance Corporation, which made loans to distressed banks and also bought stock in 6,000 banks, at a cost of $1.3 billion. When

the economy stabilized, the U.S. government sold the stock to private investors or the banks themselves.

- The similar U.S. nationalization of railways, coal mines, and even a department store chain during World War II.
- The brief U.S. seizure in 1952 of 88 steel mills to obviate an industry-wide strike that would have crippled the Korean War effort.
- The 1984 acquisition of an 80% stake in the Continental Illinois Bank and Trust, the United States' seventh-largest bank that failed in part because of bad oil-patch loans in Oklahoma and Texas. It was deemed "too big to fail" by federal regulators, who feared wider turmoil in the financial markets. The U.S. government lost an estimated $1 billion on the bad loans it bought.
- The early 1990s financial crisis in Sweden when much of the country's banking industry was nationalized. The government bought stakes in banks and sold most of them off later.

All these examples show that while not exactly like the 2008 shambles, they contain elements of the problems and the solution. And concerning the United States, which is the key to both, it is clear that while the country celebrates a culture of laissez-faire capitalism as an economic ideal, the practice of non-government intervention has strayed when necessary. Similar dogmatic decisions are evident in many other instances of experiential non-learning in most countries, both in the political sphere and industry and commerce, as my second example will show.

As a side bar to the credit crunch, it is instructive how the two key players in this mainly Anglo-Saxon political and economic drama viewed the broad concept of Experiential Learning, in which the awareness of prior experience is key. In his final press conference on January 12, 2009—at the end of the realization phase of the crisis and the beginning of the "what to do" stage—President Bush made the following statement: "*There is no such thing as short-term history.*"[35] For a man who was making history at every turn, his belief that it is a function of only time displaced must count as another of his obtuse commentaries. Six years earlier, Tony Blair, Mr. Bush's contemporary in the lead up to the crash, dispensed the following wisdom: *"A study of history provides so little instruction for our present day."* [36] The observation was made halfway through his term in office.

While the credit crisis represents one weighty enough example of experiential non-learning, the other huge exemplar, albeit with its cost spread over a much longer period, is the strategy of subsidizing post-colonial Africa, a price with at least a trillion or two dollars attached to the tag at today's rates—and with little perceptible benefit.

The non-learning aspect relates to how every other developed and developing country has emerged from their feudal pasts—by basing their advancement on the employment of individual property rights. By ignoring this essential lesson, even neglecting to insist on recipient countries adopting less medieval attitudes toward land in return for their financial help, the international "aid industry" has not only wasted money unnecessarily but also allowed one of the world's most long-running tragedies to persist.

Indeed, when the history of modern Africa is written, economic historians will be asking several uncomfortable questions. Why, over more than 50 years, did the aid industry not learn from its own experiences? Even, why it did not learn from the tried and tested experience of every other developed country?

While private land ownership is not the only reason why Africa is in its mess—high-leaching top soil and resident life-threatening diseases, war are others—these questions do not detract from the underlying issue of why post colonial Africa has, itself, resisted the lesson of others' experience. Like the instinctive standpoint of the United States toward socialism, the conventional attitude by African politicians toward agricultural land is that it is communal. But behind this apparently irreversible position there is another, less altruistic standpoint—the self-protective policy of keeping tenure in state hands so that anyone who shows disloyalty to the political base can be thrown off, a variation of which was seen in Zimbabwe when white farmers were disenfranchised.

The policy to which today's Africa aspires is commonly known as lease-hold. The policy to which the developed world has adopted is freehold, which allows individuals *ownership* of the land, a distinction exemplified by Larry Summers, ex-president of Harvard who was President Clinton's last Treasury Secretary and who headed President Obama's National Economic Council: "*Ownership matters; there has never been a case in recorded history of anybody washing a rented car.*"[37]

For Africa, the move away from their traditional mindsets would be a sea change way of thinking but no more exceptional than dozens of other, equally different cultures. Yet the aid industry has resisted the opportunity to base their philanthropy on the beneficial experience of others. The shift toward freehold would help to overcome several important regional obstacles to prosperity that have dogged the continent ever since its colonists started leaving its shores more than 50 years ago.

In addition to adapting to a more modern application of land, it would help to exchange the traditional measure of African wealth—livestock, wives, and children—for a more tradable form of personal wealth that could be used as surety for borrowing and allow individuals to create an investment economy. Using leasehold, all Africa has been capable of generating are, by and large, unproductive subsistence economies.

By providing an alternative form of wealth, it would also reduce the instinctive drive for huge families and the related tragedy of HIV AIDS. This would help to put economies on a more direct path to self-sufficiency and, in the process, reduce the burden on the West's aid industry, which has pumped in around seven post-WWII Marshall Plans over the past half century. Equal to estimates up to several trillion dollars at today's rates,[38] this largesse was expected to rise by a further $47 billion by 2010 excluding the billions in unconditional cheap loans from China.

The switch out of feudal economies is a prescription outlined in a recently published book titled *Saving Africa!* by John Hollaway. In it, the author explains that the continent has not adapted its survival mechanisms to modern times. In a straight-talking and politically incorrect account of failure, he says that throwing money at Africa had done little except encourage massive corruption, which Africans now also deem as their right (they call it "rent seeking," which the Ethiopian prime minister has publicly admitted was the "*centrepiece*" of African economies[39]), and a chronic dependency culture.

Overall in Africa there is private land ownership in some cities but virtually nothing in rural areas except in South Africa, which is busy deciding how it can revert. English-speaking countries have the most while land occupancy in French- and Portuguese-speaking regions is mainly leasehold. Generally, governments of whichever colonial origin can declare arrangements void (as did Zimbabwe), so subsistence farming is all that occurs. Evoking Larry Summers, land—Hollaway insists—must not be communal. Leasehold may provide *access*, but it does not bestow *ownership*, he adds.

Hollaway's answer is to experientially learn from the rest of the developed world as well as China, which has belatedly allowed peasants qualified ownership of their land. All have used individual property rights as the basis of their development by providing a bottom-up source of wealth. Subsistence plots could be bought, sold, and consolidated into more commercial operations capable of feeding urban populations. Then, with the means acquired, jobs could be generated. Importantly, the cycle is self-generating and wealth is not dependent on the favor—usually family- or tribe-directed—of whoever is top dog. Instructively, a similar schema was formulated by the economist Hernando de Soto and successfully introduced into Peru in the early 1990s but comparable proposals drafted for Tanzania and South Africa have been resisted, in spite of being backed by the World Bank.

For his roadmap, he suggests that, because of Africa's xenophobia, Africans themselves, in particular the continent's Black diaspora, have to front the efforts to change their homeland cultures by asking their native governments to adopt freehold policies. In fact, lawmakers would be told that development assistance would be entirely dependent on citizen ownership of land. Possibly using an international agency as their initial operating umbrella, the diaspora and talented locals would be offered opportunities to train in the skills to create a marketplace for land (a central registry, a state-run escrow system, real estate agencies, etc.). Incentives would be offered for expatriates to return home, and human nature should then be left to make the best of opportunities. It would be at this stage that aid be resumed.

Pilot projects in suitably peaceful and homogeneous countries such as Mozambique and Burkina Faso would be started. If these worked, a "me too" chant elsewhere in Africa would deafen the dissent of resistant politicians.

The current financial crisis and Africa are two more examples of how important is the subject of Experiential Learning. Indeed, the costs attached to these two examples alone would suggest that education should give the discipline a priority that equates with approaches to other existing elements of management dysfunction.

These—and the other examples—paint the tarnished picture of what is happening across the business landscape—small companies, large companies, institutions of all shapes and sizes, basically all organizations that live within the flexible labor market's orbit. For those few that, luckily, are churn free, there is still the problem of short, selective and defensive memory recall by even loyal employees. Alongside a rigorous knowledge-collection process, a dedicated and thorough Experiential Learning program is an opportunity to cut out those repeated mistakes, re-invented wheels and other unlearned lessons that threaten to allow competitors to strip away past laurels.

Remember this text's reference in Chapter 2 (see Page 14) noting in the global hierarchy of competitiveness that it cost more than 40% more to perform a similar task in New Zealand than in the United States?[40] Or Chapter 4's observation by Simon Caulkin in The Observer newspaper (see Page 42) that the United Kingdom's productivity was persistently 20–30% below its competitors. Simplistic the imagery might be but imagine, then, what would happen if New Zealand and the United Kingdom (or for that matter any of the foot-draggers) raised their game, in particular how many more widgets they could sell? That's growth— in whichever political, economic, or managerial language one chooses to translate and the very thing that so many businesses and countries are desperately searching for to get themselves out of the deep hole they've dug for themselves.

CHAPTER 6

The Smart March to Wisdom

We learn through experience and experiencing, and no one teaches anyone anything. This is as true for the infant moving from kicking to crawling to walking as it is for the scientist with his equations. If the environment permits it, anyone can learn whatever he chooses to learn; and if the individual permits it, the environment will teach him everything it has to teach

—Eric Hoffer, US philosopher[1]

EBM's 6-Stage Learning Cycle

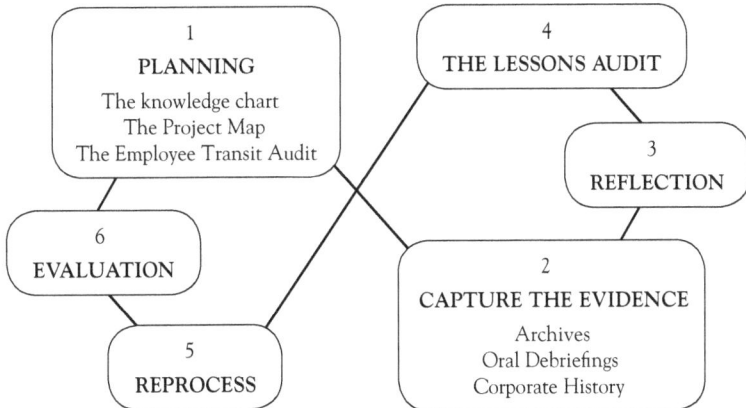

Figure 6.1. *Experience-Based Management's (EBM) continuous spiral similar to David Kolb's model of experiential learning, with the extra phases to accommodate modern working practices.*

As this text has explained, institution-specific Experiential Learning in these times of short employee tenure has to involve the capture of short-, medium- and long-term OM, its critical review alongside one's employers' stored data, information and knowledge, one's own and others' experience, and a subsequent process of reasoned deduction to arrive at so-called wisdom with which to tailor bespoke decisions for changed circumstances.

In its own 6-stage schema, **Experience-Based Management (EBM)** arrives at Professor David Kolb's model with a lot more preparation to improve the memory component of the process and a plan to preselect and capture prime experiences from which the institution needs to learn. Thereafter comes Kolb's reflection process, the decision-taking stage, the building of lessons learned to onpass to the next generation and, finally, a reprocessing exercise to rehearse and evaluate determinations to professionalise the decision making approach.

EBM's 6-stage learning cycle (Figure 6.1) incorporates the following:

- **Stage 1**: A Planning Stage to prune the potential learning opportunities down to a manageable size that harmonizes with the organization's perceived requirements. This phase incorporates the Knowledge Chart, the Project Map, and the Employee Transit Audit.
- **Stage 2**: A Capture-the-Evidence Stage to ensure that experiences do not walk out of the front door and that OM, when it is recalled, is not imprecise. This addresses the little-used mediums of Corporate History and Oral Debriefing.
- **Stage 3**: A Reflection Module to make sense of information, extract meaning, and relate this to everyday organizational and wider business life, alongside one's own and others' experience.
- **Stage 4**: A Lessons Audit to allow for institution-wide fertilization across the organization and down the generations so that learning becomes more corporate based.
- **Stage 5**: A Reprocessing Stage to test lessons learned on a range of scenarios.
- **Stage 6**: An Evaluation Stage to confirm the quality of decision making, leading to continuous learning.

Stage 1: Planning

Given that lessons are technically buried in *anything* that a business or other type of organization does, where does one start? That management dilemma of deciding how to apportion *actual* work and *learning* to work is never resolved, but the hit list of nominations for the latter can at least be trimmed by an intelligent selection of priorities.

The first step is to decide where in an organization its knowledge lies. This ferreting exercise is called the **Knowledge Chart**, which in essence is an institution's informal ranking in importance of *occupational* positions. This approach is comparable with the conventional methodology known as knowledge mapping with one important difference. Traditional knowledge mapping's objective is to discover the location of existing explicit knowledge within an organization, usually in knowledge storage technologies such as databases or physical archives. This would include its intellectual property such as patents, copyrights, trademarks, brands, registered design, trade secrets, and processes whose ownership is granted to the company by law, licensing and partnering agreements, and rules and procedures contained in process manuals. This also includes important documents, files, systems, policies, directories, competencies, relationships, and authorities. While important to decision making in its own right, the approach of EBM's Knowledge Chart is to also identify the living, breathing, and *occupant* holders of specific knowledge—those who are still accessible in the organization. This should include both managers and their key operatives. The reason for this is to identify the main decision making points where the organization can access its important tacit knowledge and experience rather than just whatever explicit knowledge is lodged within the organization's archive. In companies of up to 100 employees, such numbers of employees might add up to 15; in larger organizations this might add up to 100 or more.

With this information in hand, the next stage is to identify a list of main activities or "events/experiences" that are considered key to the organization's business. This is the so-called **Project Map**, which akin to the Knowledge Chart's hit list of knowledge sources, is intended to identify the organization's main "actions."

Depending on the institution, these might include anything the organization considers could be improved upon—for example, where quality could be enhanced and/or the cost could be reduced. This could apply to everything from a group rationalization to a new product launch and the way capital was raised from the bank or a new investor, from an employee strike to how a new manufacturing outsource company is selected or the employment of university graduates. In their selection, identification should be on the basis of an audited result (e.g., the latest product launch was twice as expensive as last year's product launch) or should be important in its own right (e.g., how a marketing campaign or a salesman managed to persuade a previously reluctant potential client to switch allegiances). The choice should also include repeatable events where the time scale of recurrence is more than the average tenure of the main decision makers and/or from work areas that have a particularly high rate of employee turnover. Additionally, organizations should select both successes and failures although it should be kept in mind that more can usually be learned from the latter than the former.

Development projects such as new product design, outsourcing enquiries, and investigations into new institutional practices are a particularly good source of learning because they are a microcosm of the whole organization. Since project teams are usually made up of people from many parts of the organization, development projects test the strengths and weaknesses of systems, structure, and values. Project auditing, especially when done only to ensure compliance with formal procedures rather than to analyze its positive and negative aspects, is invariably a lost opportunity.

To each of these activities or events/experiences is then added the name or names of the main decision makers. When choices are made, selections should not be confined only to management as lessons learned can often be just as valuable to an organization when they emanate on the shop floor. In any event, managers should also have an intimate awareness of operational issues before any decision making exercise.

The final roll call of individuals and projects to be targeted for knowledge capture is then determined after an analysis to plot the organization's actual staff turnover, in order to be able to choose judiciously between what is considered important and where the greatest level of job turnover resides. If choices have to be made, it is logical to gravitate toward those whose decision makers are more peripatetic.

This is called the **Employee Transit Audit**, which can be undertaken relatively easily by an organization's human resources/personnel department. Designed to plot the level of job discontinuity across an organization at regional, functional, and departmental levels, it is an analysis of an organization's employee turnover and, particularly, its occupational positions. Not all of the lost occupational appointments will be jobs where the knowledge loss is critical but this exercise will provide a first-level gauge of the scale of the underlying problem of staff churn.

Having identified the potential size and location of the knowledge leaks, the next job is to compare all three analyses—a job best undertaken by a senior manager in consultation with the person or persons who will eventually manage the knowledge-capture process. Where posts and names replicate will help to pinpoint priorities. From there it becomes a process of matching perceived importance with a budget to arrive at a definitive **Knowledge Retrieval Plan** that identifies events/activities and candidates for knowledge capture.

For a medium-size organization, this list might include a dozen posts that have a particularly high level of turnover. Alongside this might be another dozen events/activities, each of which identifies three or four main decision makers and key operatives. In addition, the organization might, for example, identify the chairman, chief executive, and finance director. Space in the budget could be left for several additional unexpected events and departures.

Budget is always a thorny issue. How much is organization-specific knowledge worth to stockpile and learn from—10%, 15%, 20% of an individual manager's annual salary? A percentage of the value of a project/event? The estimate of the cost of a mistake that gets repeated continuously, of wheels that are reinvented time and time again, and of change that takes an inordinate amount of time to realize? Or even the cost and time of firefighting? The value that organizations put on this esoteric commodity invariably provides a nuclear indicator whether or not they are genuine learning organizations. For many, knowledge is just an all-purpose article of trade that can be acquired simply by hiring. For them, their organization-specific experiences and knowledge are of little value. For the others, it represents the potential added value of not having to relearn their own experiences or repeat past mistakes.

The Knowledge Retrieval Plan will consist of a list of individuals and events, and a schedule of when the "capture" exercise might or should take place. For specified jobs, for example, the knowledge owners who leave with short notice should be scheduled for knowledge capture in the last month of their employment. For the specified events, the date and duration of the event will be specified along with the names of the relevant knowledge owners and decision makers, with a related timetable for knowledge retrieval—whether it be before its conclusion or after its end. For key appointments like the chairman or chief executive officer, knowledge acquisition might be scheduled in a specified non-busy period before the New Year.

Like the Project Map and the Knowledge Chart, the Employee Transit Audit and the Knowledge Retrieval Plan should be repeated on a 12-month cycle or, in the case of a seasonal business, a 6-month cycle. A low-cost exercise, it is an essential part of the overall cycle that can better target many of the organization's learning opportunities.

Stage 2: Capture the Evidence

This section does not address the processes around conventional archives or digital databases. They are dealt with in a raft of other texts and, generally, handled professionally, at least in their logistical contexts. Nor does it address the discipline known as benchmarking, which is also covered competently in other literature. It deals specifically with the widely unexploited processes alongside the capture mediums that address the overlooked component of efficient decision making and the disregarded effects of corporate amnesia. They are tacit knowledge and experience, the wider knowledge dispersal problems arising from the departure of important knowledge holders and the inherent short, selective, and defensive memories of non-mobile employees that—alongside conventional archival material—constitute institutional-specific OM.

For the capture vehicle suitable for short- and medium-term OM—**Oral Debriefings**—interviews should be undertaken around important projects and key decision makers. For an indication of how adept the collection of tacit knowledge needs to be, this author's own graphic description is the pea under the mattress and the pile of soft quilts on which the princess slept in the classic fairy tale by Hans Christian Andersen, which means that its character is buried, hidden, and difficult for individuals to articulate personally. To access it requires interviewing skills that strip away the many layers of bedcovers, effectively teasing out the erstwhile hidden and complex knowledge buried in the recesses of individuals' and organizations' skills and experiences. In the right hands, the tool is powerful and the medium is friendly. Like the tears that come from peeling a raw onion, tacit knowledge can pour out.

In practice, there are four types of oral debriefing. The ***biographical debriefing*** focuses on an individual's life or career. Conducted at stages during or at the end of an individual's career, it is usually directed at very senior officers, people with decisive effects on organizational development. Its educational value to the organization is important because it can provide industry- and organization-specific insights into such aspects as culture, values, and the way strategy would have altered over time alongside a changing marketplace. Separately, it also doubles as a motivator to successive generations.

The second type—the ***subject debriefing***—concentrates on obtaining knowledge about a single event or topic, such as a product launch or new building development, where research may require interviews with several people to obtain complete coverage. Its application is valuable when project performance is often over budget or overdue. Importantly, debriefings should take place as soon after the event as possible while the experience is still fresh in the mind. Even better, it should take place before anyone can put a value judgment on the outcome, a strategy that automatically defuses any inherent defensiveness on the part of the individual decision makers. The technique can be further modified if the organization's culture is considered excessively defensive. In this case, debriefings should take place *while* the experience is taking place. In effect, events can be assessed in real time as opposed to hindsight, not unlike the principle of the black box flight recorder that is installed in all modern aircraft; if something goes amiss, the real-time data that it stores within itself can be used to find out what went wrong. At a stroke it improves the qualitative character of the evidential input and the learning potential of the subsequent analysis.

Thirdly, there is the ***critical incident debriefing***, which, as it suggests, occurs when there is an unexpected event, usually something damaging. Such examples might include a product recall or an unfavorable item of publicity. In this event, debriefings should be carried out soon after the episode and include as many of the people involved as possible.

Finally, there is the ***exit debriefing***, commonly known as the exit interview, which is ordinarily not an interview at all, rather the output of a formulaic, 20-questions means of trying to uncover reasons why employees leave. When done well in oral, non-questionnaire format, however, the debriefing can center on the issues and decisions unique to the exiting individual's job and can be especially instructive as a decision making tool. With senior decision makers being the most common candidates, such debriefings are always conducted near the end of a person's tenure. Although also related to subject interviews, they are often categorized separately because they may cover many topics.

To secure employee cooperation, collaborative understandings can be included in all new contracts of employment.

To the unskilled, interview techniques have typically been those used by journalists, where interviewees are consciously focused on the present. To be really fruitful, the discipline needs to concentrate more intensely on the "pea" of Hans Christian Andersen's princess's shrewd mother if it is to be applied as a decision making tool.

The choice of a skilled interviewer is essential, mainly because the spoken word is invariably a more efficient way of conveying the abstract and complex nature of elements like the nuances of corporate culture, management style, and the often-obscure issues surrounding decision making within groups. Whether the choice of individual is in-house or external the person in charge of the debriefing needs to be commanding enough not to be intimidated by the interviewee and insightful enough to identify and pursue pertinent questions. The actual skill of oral debriefing is the art of asking relevant questions and when the answers are unclear or fudged, the asking of even more probing questions. In many respects, the questioner is the more important component for, when left to his or her own devices, the subject's contribution is typically bland and lacking both incisiveness and rigor.

In addition to being a good questioner, the person in charge of the debriefing needs to be an even better listener, for a large part of the debriefing is in the asking of supplementary questions when the interviewee's responses are unclear, imprecise, or evasive. Also, a well-prepared questioner will be aware of gaps and inconsistencies in the available source materials and will ask questions to clarify or, in some instances, confirm the record. Such responses might shed new light on an issue or serve as yardsticks to judge the accuracy of other information provided by the interviewee. It is here that most tacit knowledge resides.

The medium of oral debriefing as a knowledge-capture device is, in fact, not new; nor is its application as a learning tool. Oral debriefing's first big cheerleader and practitioner was the American social commentator and writer Studs Terkel. Born in 1912, his fascination with the medium came soon after the tape recorder's commercial exploitation, when he started interviewing a whole cross-section of American society to piece together a jigsaw puzzle of experiences. In one of his best-selling books,[2] Terkel makes his own observation about collecting oral history, including its importance in the work environment: *"Amnesia is much easier to come by. As technology has become more hyperactive, we, the people, have become more laid back; as the deposits in its memory banks have become more fat, the deposits in man's memory bank have become more lean. Like [Harold] Pinter's servant, the machine has assumed the responsibilities that were once the master's. The latter has become the shell of a once thoughtful, though indolent, being. It is the Law of Diminishing Enlightenment at work. Oral history is an extremely rich source for exploring the past and present of organizations. The stories managers and workers tell about their organizations are useful diagnostic tools."*

Terkel's pioneering work was concurrent with the efforts of the U.S. academic Professor Allan Nivens who, after successfully persuading educationalists to introduce oral history as a tool for serious scholarship in the 1940s, founded the Oral History Collection at Columbia University. Since then, other universities, including Harvard, Princeton, and the University of California—Berkeley, have also developed extensive collections of oral history. In the early 1950s Nivens brought oral history to industry when he organized the interview of more than 400 people for a history of the Ford Motor Company. *"In the hands of a skilled professional, oral history can bring management helpful information, perspective, and insight,"* he says. *"It can benefit managers coping with the pace of change in the modern economy and the short-lived nature of the corporate memory. Oral history can supply that memory and needed perspectives in making decisions."* Since then a handful of companies have supported similar programs, among them ARCO, Beckman Instruments, Bristol-Myers, Eli Lilley, Kaiser Aluminum and Chemical, Monsanto, Proctor & Gamble, Rohm and Haas, and Standard Oil Company.

These were the exceptions. Since industry broadly continued to ignore oral history's employment as a capture vehicle or even as a decision making tool, the main thrust of the discipline then transferred to the U.S. military, where it was seen as an essential means of preserving the experiences of past battles and of imparting those experiences to younger soldiers. Since WWII oral history—also known as "after-action reviews"—has become an increasingly critical adjunct to the more traditional sources of historical documentation.

For example, the army decided to play a more significant role in telling its own story of WWII. A former journalist, Lieutenant Colonel (later Brigadier General) S.L.A. Marshall, was assigned to pioneer the army's oral history effort, which subsequently involved several hundred soldier-historians. Moving freely about the battle lines to gather interviews, their collection process began either while units were still in action or up to 10 days or more after the action. A special collection of interviews provided a *"view from the other side"*[3] when captured German and Japanese general officers were debriefed in order to provide intelligence information on successful combat tactics as well as useful historical material. These was usually different from strategic interrogations.

Improved techniques were employed in the Korean War and, later, in the Vietnam War, as well as the United States' military deployments to Grenada, Panama, Southwest Asia, and, more recently, Afghanistan and the Gulf. As a sign of the growing importance of oral history in the army, in 1970 Army Chief of Staff General William C. Westmoreland directed the U.S. Army War College and the U.S. Army Military History Institute to sponsor jointly what has become known as the Senior Officer Oral

History Program. The program, designed to allow most retired officers to convey to younger officers the qualities and experiences that made their careers successful, has produced more than 100,000 transcribed pages. Adopted by the navy in 1969, there exists in the U.S. Naval Institute's Oral History program alone more than 200 bound volumes, and interviews have been done to produce dozens more.

Expanding the range of army oral history activities, the U.S. Army Corps of Engineers established an active biographical and subject interview program in 1977. This was extended in the early 1980s at most of the U.S. Army Training and Doctrine Command's centers and schools. Today, in each army major command (MACOM), interviews collect data for preparing monographs or to teach lessons learned to young soldiers. In 1986 the Department of the Army directed that those exit interviews—called End of Tour (EoT) interviews—also be conducted with departing school commandants as well as division, corps, and MACOM commanders, to make interviews available to incoming commanders so that they can better understand the issues faced by their predecessors. In the late 1980s the Center of Military History went even further by creating an Oral History Activity to coordinate issues concerning all of the army's oral history programs.

The laudatory comments of Terkel and Nivens aside, the value of oral debriefing can be judged by the more recent comments of Jochen Kraske,[4] head of the World Bank Group Historical Office, who admits that even though most company work processes are largely designed around documentation, much remains unrecorded. Decisions taken, especially those regarding policies, are not always reflected in the files: *"The voluminous paper record may provide no more than bare facts, and even that record often reflects the desire to gloss over disagreements and serious questions, or the desire to sell or excuse. An additional vital source of information is the views and perceptions of those who participated in the decision making processes. We can learn much about what happened and why by asking those involved when a loan was identified and appraised, a crucial policy decision taken, a particular contract awarded."*

An effective oral history program, he says, *"can address the problem of this gap by recording, before time dilutes or erases them, the memories of executive directors, borrowers, managers and staff, who participate in key events and developments in the bank's evolution. Catching and questioning key participants in important decisions before time takes its toll will do much to fill in the record."*

The bank's experience, he adds, is also of interest to policy makers, development practitioners, and academic communities in both developing and advanced countries, who look to it to throw light on what was done, and whether it worked, thus helping—they hope—to avoid the errors of the past. With the passage of time, and as older staff retire, there has been a loss of institutional memory. It is easy today to be unaware of what happened yesterday on important issues. Staff often learn of the past, if they learn it at all, accidentally or incidentally, in a fragmentized fashion. Without the history, new staff in particular may be missing an important component of institutional culture—of understanding what the bank is and how it got there.

For the other capture medium, **Corporate Histories**—the source of long-term OM—this author's usual recommendation is that they should be updated every 5 years. And for organizations that are uncomfortable about wider exposure of their histories, the advice is that the documentation be kept private, even unpublished.

The biggest hurdle is for organizations to be nursed away from hagiography and toward a serious document of record that can be constructively used as a development tool for staff and managers in particular. This requires a format that gives the document authoritative content, which invariably requires a suitably qualified author with good editorial backup from the start. The counsel is that projects should be managed independently using an academic or professional researcher and a professional writer, the former to contribute rigor and credence to the project and the latter to add the necessary element of readability. To bestow independence and credibility, it is important for the author to be allowed to retain his or her copyright.

A good project manager should be able to bring to the project a number of distinctive skills not usually available if done in-house:

- Advise on the best editorial structure and build this into a working set of objectives
- Headhunt a suitable author and researcher

- Construct the contractual arrangements between the author/researcher and the project manager/publisher and the subject company and the project manager/publisher
- Manage on a day-to-day basis the author, researcher, and subject company to ensure momentum is maintained and deadlines achieved and provide monthly reports to the subject company
- Edit the manuscript
- Broker any changes that need to be made to the manuscript
- Publish according to the subject company's requirements
- If the subject organization wants to externalize the manuscript, market, sell, and distribute the book

With the author and subject company distanced from the subject organization, the resultant manuscript/book should ensure that a subject company's long-term memory has the necessary authority for powerful applications beyond public relations.

In spite of these endorsements, it is instructive that few business schools use all-embracing corporate or management chronicles in their curricula. One reason is the dearth of suitable accounts, leaving the responsibility for their production and application to institutions themselves. If business schools cannot or will not use corporate/management history in their curricula, they should at least teach how; if institutions make them available to employees, they can be applied as a decision making tool. This is exemplified by the attitude towards the official history of ICI, once one of United Kingdom's biggest companies, which was written by a non-academic, the late Bill Reader, who is acknowledged as being one of United Kingdom's finest of its modern corporate historians. In it[5]—a work that even academic business historians describe as one of the best and most readable of the genre—there is a classic account of insider dealing in the 1930s of how individuals speculated massively against the company. According to Dr Richard Davenport-Hines, a former editor of the journal *Business History:* "*Nobody's ever cited it as an event ever since. No one knows about it because few have ever read the book. They can't have done because the documentation in the story that Reeder got through is stunning.*"[6]

Stage 3: Reflection

Having the historic evidence of one's own as well as one's new employers' experience is not sufficient to help make good and better decisions. Any new decision still has to be adapted to new circumstances, whereby old knowledge is transformed into new knowledge, and where the component of wisdom is created. This is where the learning component of Experiential Learning has to take place, beginning with a Reflection phase that involves recalling and interpreting the experiences and understanding the relationships of events using both individual memory and *all* the organization's repositories. Preferably in a group situation consisting of all the decision makers involved, the pre-selected learning opportunities identified in Stage 1 are examined as soon after the event as possible, with decision makers stepping back from task involvement to review what actually happened. Whether or not to involve learners in role play or live or video demonstrations is optional but this practitioner's own experience is that theatrics or a TV presenter's skills are not very high on most managers' list of personal competencies. However, unceremonious and off-the-record discourse *is* desirable, so the oral delivery of case studies or testimonies is often a more productive way of initiating the reflection and conceptualization phases. Depending on individual personalities and the group dynamics of project teams, there are several approaches that can be used.

One is for individuals to orally deliver detailed chronological diaries of how their particular decisions were made, explaining the justifications at each critical determination point. Depending on the complexity of the decision, individuals should be encouraged to deliver their testimonies of their decision making process in as short a time as possible, perhaps even with a pre-designated time limit—a discipline that should enhance memory processes, hone observational scrutiny, enrich both language and communication skills, and reveal ingrained attitudes and beliefs. Their reminiscences should be based on the evidence that can be recalled from their memory and validated in the archive and their oral debriefings, including those of their main operatives, the content of which provides the decision maker with a co-existing shop floor perspective. Another approach is for individuals to allow themselves to be questioned by their decision making associates about the chronology and justifications for their determinations. Both approaches provide an evidence-rich and rigorous method for individuals to orally muse their way through something as complex as decision making. Even timelines of exactly what managers did and when can often be very revealing.

It is important that the depositions refer to historical precedent with an emphasis on precedent *within* the organization as well as to relevant theory and other decision making approaches, such as the Decision Tree. Learners are encouraged by the facilitator to make sense of the information and extract meaning for both themselves and their employer (and, if relevant, society as a whole), in particular to identify patterns of behavior and outcomes, even formulating their own theories. By reviewing the chosen experience from as many perspectives as possible, the learners are encouraged to put the experiences into some sort of overview in an organization-, job-, and person-specific context. In the case of strategy-type issues, it would be important to also consult the repository of long-term OM, the organization's corporate history, and even others' corporate histories.

Stage 4: The Lessons Audit

To oblige the decision making skew, the next stage involves learners jointly evaluating how their prior decisions could have been different in the *exact* historical circumstances of the time—specifically how, using the benefit of hindsight, their changed decisions could have elicited a more productive outcome. This culminates in a jointly written list of lessons specific to the chosen experience—a so-called **Lessons Audit**, the objective being to produce a hit list of dos and don'ts, and other counsel for consideration next time an experience of a similar nature arises. The lessons are broken down into strategy-type conclusions and operational-type suppositions. With a suitable preface, the Lessons Audit then becomes a definitive notice of new knowledge with which the organization can pass on to selected others, both those within the company and new entrants when they arrive, with a note that this erudition should provide the *starting point* for their own decision making process. This practitioner likes to describe this as "leg-up," or the means by which new knowledge can be shared across the organization and down the generations efficiently.

Stage 5: Reprocessing

Learners then orally test the lessons of Stage 4 on a variety of different scenarios such as changed raw material circumstances, increased competition, lack of finance and specified outside regulation, and so on—the circumstances that managers *think* may be the upcoming decision making variables. For this, it is useful to draw on the predictions of industry economists and other analysts, whose opinions can be brought in but are often found in the newspages of responsible newspapers and journals. Individuals effectively predict what is likely to happen in the future and then suggest what actions should be taken to refine the way both the prior determination and the *refined* determination—the one that was reprocessed in Stage 4's Lessons Audit—might be taken. It is a decision making rehearsal, out of which emerges the more rigorous ability for managers to make determinations that are based on the tried-and-tested past and to be applied beneficially to the less unfamiliar future.

In this phase it is helpful to attach a figurative word picture to the different scenarios, the objective being to be as graphic as possible. For an investment adviser that changes its research and portfolio analysts at short notice, this might be like "divorcing and remarrying within the month." For a sharp sales downturn, this could be like "finding an unwelcome relative in the spare bedroom with a dozen suitcases and 12 mislaid suitcase keys." To top managers, a succession of senior defections could be like "finding oneself in a room full of familiar strangers" while a glitch in a new product development could be like "a confectioner without any baking powder." The purpose of this exercise is to attach an informal and personal interpretation to the different events that challenge the learner to be thoughtful and inventive. It also provides a way for the episode to be disconnected from the customary use of dry facts and figures that characterize most self-assessments. By associating events more familiarly, the occurrences and their associated decisions become more contextually memorable, a device similar to how some people recall the names of new acquaintances.

A useful exercise at this stage is for managers to devise a decision making schema to *deliberately* achieve a downturn similar to the performance that the organization wants to improve. For example, if a recent product launch came out overdue and over budget by a factor of two, managers then proactively work out the decisions necessary to achieve this lower outcome in the new circumstances anticipated for the next product launch. The discipline of trying *not* to improve is frequently educational in its own right, providing as it does a direct comparison with the proposed approach to *correct* prior performance.

Stage 6: Evaluation

In this stage begins the real-time application of OM, the process of turning old knowledge into new knowledge. It is this formulation that provides one of several more knowledge platforms that provide other opportunities for even better Experiential Learning.

The first is when an event of a similar nature to the chosen experience in Stage 3 arises. Learners then retrieve the devised lessons of Stage 4 and, using the dummy run knowledge acquired in Stage 5, reinterpret the knowledge to oblige their employer's new circumstances.

After a decision has been taken but before it is implemented, the decision maker justifies concisely the determination *in writing* with an institution-specific precedent (if possible) and an accompanying rationalization under the basic headings "The Decision," "How," and "Why." Citing precedent will provide evidence that the decision has been made contextually while the complementary justification imparts the necessary attendant conceptualization, useful (with the earlier Stage 4 Learning Audit) for further Experiential Learning down the line. It also averts later memory lapse and, if learning is actively championed by the employer, encourages managers to be less defensive than they might otherwise be—an important component of discovery and new knowledge.

Even then, this is not the end of the learning process. After the outcome becomes measurable, they use the loop again to assess whether revised practice can be turned into even better practice, in which case the *Learning Audit* can be updated again. In the multilinked chain of evolution, explicit knowledge has become tacit knowledge and then has become explicit knowledge again. In essence, old knowledge has become new knowledge available to be reapplied—a process that supports the universal paradigm of progress being incremental and learning being continuous.

In addition to using prior experience as a tool to assess the many variants of decision making ahead and behind actual events, the logic of the EBM Learning Loop is to make continual incremental improvements to real business situations. The more often reflection is undertaken, the more frequently the opportunity arises to modify and refine decision making to better effect. On the basis that if one waits until after a task is completed, there is no opportunity to refine it until a similar task arises; there is also the option of starting the reflection stage *before* an experience is completed.

It may all sound like an elaborate process, but then, management was never intended to be uncomplicated or effortless. In truth, it is already tortuous and not as successful as it could be. The argument is that it is better to get the front end of decision making right and make improvements than to spend as much, or even more, energy, time and money on the remedial end of the exercise.

The plan is to travel the straightest possible line to get to a desired destination, which is the whole point and goal of Experiential Learning and the better management of its leading co-conspirator, OM. The urgency of Peter Drucker's productivity call, and especially productivity *growth*, is KM's bigger and better role. It's what the business dogfight is all about.

CHAPTER 7

How the Baton was Passed

If the past cannot teach the present and the father cannot teach the son, then history need not have bothered to go on, and the world has wasted a great deal of time

—Russell Hoban, U.S. author[1]

Conceptions are usually one person's exclusive output, but their development is nearly always organic—the building of one bit of understanding upon another, exactly like the theoretical model of Experiential Learning itself. Even this one.

The genus of the idea, which focuses on how people learn, has its origins in the field of psychology, philosophy, and physiology, not education or industry. In the first half of the 20th century, so-called behaviorialism—a Pavlovian view of human behavior[2]—dominated the field. Without knowledge of what was going on in the brain, scientists limited their theories to aspects of stimulus and response, a view that eventually spilled over into other disciplines such as education, sociology, and even linguistics.

First on the scene was Jean Piaget, the Swiss philosopher and psychologist, who spent much of his professional life listening to growing children.[3] In the course of his work with the Frenchman Alfred Binet, the creator of the first intelligence test, he became interested in the reasoning process used by those performing intelligence tests. He found that there were age-related regularities in the reasoning processes as well as differences in the way children thought about things. These insights led him to undertake a study of experience and human knowledge. Over a near 70-year working life, Piaget's pioneering researches in developmental psychology and genetic epistemology gave him an insight into how knowledge grows, a discovery that Albert Einstein described as *"so simple that only a genius could have thought of it.*"[4] What Piaget realized was that children were not empty vessels to be filled with knowledge, as traditional educational theory believed, but rather they were active builders of knowledge through the continuous creation and testing of their own perceived theories of the world. It was an understanding in the field that others would later develop such individualistic teaching approaches in their own right, among them the Italian medical doctor and educator Maria Montessori, whose ideas have spawned specialist schools that still bear her name around the world.

Further refinement was initiated by the likes of American academic Jack Mezirow, who introduced the idea of transformative learning; the U.S. philosopher and psychologist John Dewey,[5] whose concern was with "*interaction, reflection, and experience*"; the Brazilian educationalist Paulo Freire,[6] whose methodology introduced "*dialogue*" into the learning process; and the German-born psychologist Kurt Lewin,[7] who brought to the table the concept of action research, a form of collective self-reflective enquiry.

Dewey's contribution—education must engage with and enlarge experience through interaction and reflection—came out of the observation that traditional teaching was teacher driven, where the chief business of a school was to transmit to the new generation "*bodies of information and of skills that had been worked out in the past.*" From this he re-conceptualized vocational teaching to be learner centered. Dewey rejected knowledge of the past as the end of education—rather, he said, it is a means. For educators, the challenge was how to use experience to educate, the subject of this text.

Lewin's contribution was the realization that learning was best facilitated in an environment where there is dialectic tension and conflict between concrete experience and analytic detachment. Like Dewey, Lewin became convinced that the way to understand anything was to understand experience's evolution.

This changed the Pavlovian view of personal growth to more cognitive and humanist theories, which spawned Benjamin Bloom's work[8] with the hierarchical nature of knowledge, Abraham Maslow's ideas[9] on how learners attempt to take control of their own life processes, Robert Gagne's identification[10] of the main categories of learning, and the Chris Argyris–Donald Schön collaboration[11] that innovated the groundbreaking methodology known as double-loop learning.

The Argyris-Schön starting point for many learners is in the detection and correction of errors within governing variables such as given or chosen goals, values, plans, and rules—what is recognized as incremental or single-loop learning. Learning is usually limited to new skills and capabilities, with applications in quality problems. Usually based on negative feedback, it involves doing something better without necessarily examining or challenging underlying beliefs and assumptions. In contrast, double-loop or reframing learning is the process of questioning governing variables with a view to changing the organization's underlying norms, policies, and objectives and is oriented toward professional education, especially leadership in organizations. It often embraces single-loop learning but takes the process a stage further by fundamentally reshaping the underlying patterns of thinking and behavior through reflection and self-analysis. Through this process, routines, thinking, and behavior outside an individual's level of conscious awareness are exposed, enabling individual and organizational change. While acknowledging the importance of experience, there was still no adequate theory as to experience's precise function in learning. Experience was still seen as a source of stimuli—until Roger Saljo[12] observed that the more life experience students had, the more likely they were to view learning as an internal, experience-based process. His hierarchy of student views of learning concluded that learning increased knowledge; that it involved storing information for easy recall; and that it was about developing skills and methods, acquiring facts that could be used as necessary, making sense of information, extracting meaning, and relating information to everyday life. In summary, it was about understanding the world through re-interpreting knowledge, which confirmed the earlier models of learning and cognitive development that said that intelligence was shaped by experience and that intelligence was not an innate, internal characteristic but rather a product of the interaction between individuals and their environment.

Nonetheless, although the concept was recognized and up-and-running, the theory of Experiential Learning did not gain prominence until the work of Jack Mezirow,[13] Paulo Freire, Anthony Gregorc,[14] and Carl Rogers[15] in the 1980s who stressed that the focal point of all learning lies in the way experience is processed, in particular in its critical reflection. They spoke of learning as a cycle that begins with experience, continues with reflection, and later leads to action, which itself becomes a concrete experience available for the next round of reflection.

Mezirow's transformative learning was conceived in a groundbreaking study of women who returned to community college to continue their education while Freire's main work concerned popular and informal education through conversational rather than a curricula form, where educational activity was situated in the actual experience of participants. Others have contributed, among them Swiss-born Etienne Wenger,[16] a pioneer of "community of practice" groups; German-born Fritz Perls,[17] one of the originators of Gestalt therapy; the Australian George Elton Mayo,[18] who became an early leader in the field of industrial sociology in the United States emphasizing the dependence of productivity on small-group unity; and American Peter Senge,[19] who introduced The Learning Organization and systems thinking to the world in 1990. Advocating reflectiveness as part of the learning process, Senge's focus was on decentralizing the role of leadership to enhance the capacity of employees to work more productively. There is even a newer model called triple-loop learning, sometimes called multiple-loop learning, which introduces an additional learning phase in order to manage organizational diversity by helping individuals create a shift in personal perceptions through the questioning of inconsistencies and incongruence in organizations.

All of these reformers' approaches have led to four different learning processes, all of which are overlapping. Action-driven approaches, explored by the likes of academics Reg Revans,[20] Argyris, Schön,[21] and Wenger, emphasize the behavioral changes that take place when managers solve organizational problems. The cognition approaches of people like Robert Kegan,[22] Stephen Klein,[23] Etienne Wenger, Daniel Goleman,[24] and Peter Senge focus on ways in which managers think, specifically on individual and group thinking processes such as memory and perception, with a view to creating coherent, orderly representations of complex problems. The reflective approaches of individuals like Russ Vince,[25] Michael Reynolds,[26] Jack Mezirow, Gordon Dehler,[27] and Ann Welsh[28] focus on the process of critical reflection using historical, social, and cultural evidence while the experiential approaches of the likes of William Torbert,[29] David Kolb, Judy Le Heron,[30] and Ikujiro Nonaka[31] focus on how managers acquire and transform old knowledge into new knowledge.

But it has been David Kolb who has taken the discipline into its most refined stage, having integrated Dewey's pragmatism, Lewin's social psychology, Piaget's cognitive development, Rogers's client-centered therapy, Maslow's humanism, and Perls's Gestalt therapy. Kolb's short-hand description[32] of the concept is that learning is the process "*whereby knowledge is created through the transformation of experience.*" His model takes concrete experience through the process of observation and reflection, to the formation of abstract concepts and generalizations, and finally to testing the implications of new concepts in new situations. The experiential way of learning, he says, involves the application of the information received from the educator to the experiences of learners. It does not consist of activity generated in the classroom alone, and learners do not acquire their knowledge exclusively from the educator. Rather, they learn through the process of taking the new information derived in the classroom and testing it against their accustomed real-life experiences. The learner thus transforms both the information and the experience into knowledge of some new or familiar subject or phenomenon. In Kolb's model, the educator is a *facilitator* of a person's learning cycle.

It should be pointed that the methodology outlined in this text does not detract from Kolb's model—rather, just the aspects that can adapt it more effectively to business practice and the modern working environment.

Unlike traditional Experiential Learning, which concentrates on the application of contemporary experience, this approach introduces prior experience to the table, a feature that should open up vast new areas of scholarship for academia and would-be benefits for practicing organizations. It also extends the conventional discipline to specifically address *all* decision making through a pre-selection process that filters *in* perceived prime learning prospects. And since the flexible labor market has made OM employee resident, the focus returns this valuable intellectual asset to the employer. Experience-Based Management (EBM) then uses a portable "lessons learned" approach that can be easily moved down the high-churn generations. It is practical, allows reflective enquiry and gives KM the big-ticket application it merits to confront the dysfunction of conventional practice in both business education and in commerce and industry.

CHAPTER 8

Way to Go

It is not the strongest of the species that survives, nor the most intelligent, but the one most responsive to change.

—Charles Darwin[1]

This text has been all about learning and wisdom being organic and incremental, and productivity being one of the undervalued answers to lack of competitiveness and survival, so it is appropriate to look at what two wise men have to say about the subject of change. It is what industry, commerce, and business education have to do to their mindsets when considering how to deal with the veiled effects of the flexible labor market, corporate amnesia, and their marginalized decision-making practices.

The first comes from the man, quoted in the strapline to this chapter, above, who combined his intellect with knowledge and experience to come up with something of pure genius that keeps on confirming the progressive nature of adaptive improvement. Whilst biologically grounded, his theory of evolution also has a familiar resonance with experiential learning with an additional suggested undertone; that the learning process dictates almost all developmental capabilities and explains why those who don't learn, won't progress; why those who don't *continue* to learn, degrade; and why those who *do* learn, advance. As true for individual companies and other types of organization as well as countries, the observation does not disclose great intelligence or technical ability, but is as accurate for the likes of Zimbabwe, those laggards whose productivity growth is in the red, China, and others. But it does reveal an understanding that is only understood by the motivated.

The second quote that deals with the need for change is this text's champion of the administrative arts, Peter Drucker. In another age that goes some way to echo the current economic turmoil and the difficulty of making change[2] he said: "*Everybody has accepted by now that change is unavoidable. But that still implies that change is like death and taxes—it should be postponed as long as possible and no change would be vastly preferable. But in a period of upheaval, such as the one we are living in, change is the norm."*

As suggested, change is a much-resisted characteristic of almost everyone, no less managers and especially organizations. Take David Kolb's now more than a quarter of a century's acknowledged work on experiential learning itself. His recollection is that it only started to be recognized empirically after more than 10 years, and that decade ended in the 1980s. Its take-up since has continued to be agonizingly unhurried.

As a general observation, shifting the educational scenery has historically been very difficult, with "we know better" the typical mindset. Within this, the political arm of change is usually the most influential in a hesitant, disbelieving way. Business and other types of employers are generally defensive until their backs are up against the wall, at which point they become reactive, reluctantly. They are also quite demanding of the political and academic arms but usually patronized, especially by business academia that, whilst intellectually intimidating to all, find the business of business mostly overwhelming. All are keen payers of lip service, which is why—and dare this politically incorrect non-academic say it—that in spite of apparent overwhelming evidence of relevant teaching processes to be had, prevailing values are continually reinforced, making them all very good experiential ***non***-learners.

Because of this, the journey of change will inevitably be long, but there must come a point at which someone realizes that more has to be done; perhaps that will be when there is understanding of how corporate amnesia is disenfranchising the existing wealth-creating machine and productivity is slipping into negative territory.

The typical impression is that all this sounds like a lot of extra work. The point here, which is worth repeating, is that it is a device to enable managers to work smarter rather than longer or necessarily harder. Get more of the top-flight decisions right and less time and money will need to be spent on fire fighting.

For experiential learning to happen, there are a number of misunderstandings about the new workplace that need to be first resolved.

- Because of the changed working environment, both academics and commerce/industry need to stop seeing knowledge as employee resident. Institutional revolving doors and musical chairs have given OM a fleeting character that prescribes value to the employer *only* if it is resident within the organization and available to itinerant employees to apply.

- Employers need to realize that supporting the flexible labor market at the same time as trying to reduce job turnover is like shouting into the wind. Better to deal with the inevitable discontinuity, corporate amnesia, and poor decision as a separate issue.

- Academia and industry/commerce have to decide whether or not they really believe Henry Ford's pronouncement that "*history is more or less bunk*"[3] (it survives as one of the most often quoted aphorisms to debunk the wider subject of memoir as a learning tool). The management of OM and experiential learning has to be acknowledged as sensible educational tools, with all *parties more fully appreciating* the close relationship between the evidence of precedent and better decision making.

- Organizations should realize that failure does not provide the only learning opportunity. Success can also be improved upon.

- To overcome innate managerial defensiveness about personal and corporate performance, employers need to encourage cultures that support objective reflection without penalty. Specifically, they need to see experiential learning as less of a threat and more of an opportunity by demonstrating a corporate maturity that extends beyond the defensive posture of the insecure. On that basis, failure can be delayed success rather than an event that risks repetition.

- Industry/commerce should accept that higher productivity is as much an issue for management as it is for workface employees. In truth, high-skill employees are no substitute for poor decision making from above.

- The lessons of business and corporate history should not be the private musings of the elderly; ownership should be employer-specific, beginning with the next generation of managers. That way, the shortsighted will be able to listen to the longsighted.

- Academic KM has to admit the wider definition of experiential learning into its orbit and historians have to also see themselves as knowledge practitioners.

- Just as the detail of institutional-specific experience is essential to the preparation of conventional case studies, so too will it be central to experiential learning. As such, the device will need a continuing collaborative effort of business education and employers—arguably more than has existed in the past—if industry and commerce are to maximize the potential benefits from both the flexible labor market and institutional-specific experience.

Thereafter, someone has to decide into which bit of academic real estate experiential learning best fits. Is it business history, which has the chronological bent to document the evidence? Would they, then, be qualified to teach how to learn? Or would it more comfortably reside within KM, the Cinderella subject that part fits into computer science and/or human resources? And in terms of companies themselves, it is a role that that is unrecognizable in any existing job, so might it live in the archive, which would still be required to maintain the institutions' records, or human resources, which more often than not deals with issues of training?

Finally, it would need to be recognized in the management hierarchy. Is a manager of OM or experiential learning, deserving enough for a vocational position or the boardroom? At the end of the day much will depend on experiential learning's perceived importance alongside the fiscal size of the repeated mistakes, re-invented wheels and the other unlearned lessons that desecrate the bottom line.

Checkbooks and Boxing Gloves

Origins of the Author's Interest

History provides experience cheaply
—Leslie Hannah, the U.K.'s first
Professor of Business History[1]

This author's interest in Organizational Memory (OM) and Experiential Learning came about organically through several unconnected observations in the 1970s and 1980s whilst working for the *Financial Times* in London.

The period spanned a decade of commercial activity in the United Kingdom that registered an event—seemingly more accidental than planned—that had a seminal effect on the country's economic prospects. It happened when the majority of workers stopped being paid weekly in cash and bank accounts became the norm for the majority of citizens for the first time, a choice that had been commonplace for at least 40 years in the United States and which had been introduced in neighboring France by President Charles de Gaulle immediately after WWII. It marked the point when Britain belatedly changed itself from a cash economy into an investment economy.

Unheralded, the effect was that individuals unconsciously changed their budgeting habits from a 7-day cycle to a 30-day cycle. Rather than having to plan for a week at a time, the extra cash at the beginning of each month meant that Britons had to think in ways that encompassed interest rates and financial planning. At a stroke, money that was traditionally kept in the back pocket was issued straight into the mainstream economy through bank accounts and other forms of investment, helping to fuel Mrs. Thatcher's enterprise boom.

It was a decision that could have been made much earlier by observing and adapting the experience of others. For this author, it was his first cognisant exposure to the potential power of Experiential Learning, albeit one that emanated from others' experience and which happened much later in the country's industrial history than competing nations. To him, the puzzling aspect of this late conversion was that the United Kingdom was the world's oldest industrialized country, which should have given it a clear experiential advantage in the development stakes. Instead, it served as a *disadvantage*, turning the country into a very late player. The "why" generated many introspective discussions. The "how"—how to tackle the enigma—took much longer.

The author's role at the *Financial Times* was company commentator and specialist writer for the newspaper's Management Page, which gave him the opportunity of meeting, on an annual basis, literally hundreds of senior-ranking businessmen across the commercial spectrum. The industrial transformation could not have been more dramatic, with the period around 1980 marked by companies being mainly reactive and defensive in character. Thereafter, once the Government started demonstrating through legislation that the industrial initiative was being shifted to the boardroom, companies literally mutated before his eyes. Among the areas in which the author took a special interest were personnel, management education, management consultancy, and management itself. He also covered the early examples of companies addressing the issue of radical job changes that would herald the onslaught of downsizing and the industry-wide white-collar shakeout of older workers, outsourcing and working from home. It was the onset of the flexible labor market. In all this activity, he noticed something unusual.

In conversations with all these fast-running businessmen, it was conspicuous that the most successful had a keen historical perspective of their industries, business in general, and their own companies in particular. They were easily able to refer to precedent and incremental developments within a longer historical timeframe. In contrast, the less successful managers—defined as those whose employers either ranked below the first division of their sector or who did not seem to last very long in their jobs—were notably non-reflective about their activities to the extent that they were distinctly dismissive, even hostile, about looking back. A fairly typical response from this group of people—the majority, it seemed— would be that reflection was no more than nostalgia or sentiment, that they considered it more important to look forward, that past models didn't apply because circumstances and tools changed or that they wanted to change their culture, not perpetuate it. Often, they would insist that many decisions were taken in defiance of precedent, conveniently ignoring the associated reality that one had to know what the precedents were in order to take a contrary course. The other observation was an almost obsessive disposition to avoid admitting to—and discussing—mistakes. When it was unavoidable, the blame was invariably placed elsewhere— except by the more successful managers.

The interim conclusion the author came to at the time was that some managers probably had better public relations advisers who, one knew, were always hovering in the background. But as the anecdotal evidence built up and reinforced the author's surveillance, why, he kept asking himself, would an awareness of how one's predecessors did things—and the events they had experienced—make the difference, especially in an environment where, as his defined set of unsuccessful managers kept reminding him, circumstances seemed to change so often?

The answer did not come immediately, but it eventually struck him that business decisions were no different to decisions taken in other areas of life—better made with the benefit of hindsight.

This wasn't a particularly earth-moving moment until the author discovered just how absent hindsight was in the world of business. The author's research at the time revealed that British workers at all levels acquired little historical awareness of business from the wider educational system or the workplace. While there was a passable level of exposure in schools and universities to the 220-year-old industrial revolution and economic history dealing with macro-fiscal issues, there was a noticeable absence of corporate and business history that would familiarize the emerging generation of workers, consumers, and potential investors with how, at the practical level, their parents and grandparents earned their livings—the type of information, for example, that traced the development of companies in particular and business in general. In at least one outside survey, secondary school children, for example, could name just two British companies. It was puzzling because there was plenty of political history, social history, and military history in the curriculum to demonstrate the *bona fides* of the genre as an educational tool and as a means to reinforcing a culture. But for the people who had to go out and earn their living in the business world—that is, practically everyone—there was virtually nothing in the way of corporate or business and management history.

Apart from illustrative references—called case studies but usually no more than summarized snapshot examples used to explain the workings of some functional management disciplines—the subjects were (and still are) even neglected at business schools, where management educators were teaching the nation's future businessmen how to manage *without* the perspectives of their predecessors or an awareness of their corporate past. It was equivalent to Britain's Sandhurst, the armed forces academy that trains the nation's future military leaders, not referring to WWI, WWII, the Korean War, the Falklands, or the Gulf wars in their classrooms.

Alongside this and against the background of the accelerating demise of the job-for-life work model, very few British companies were passing down their own experiences from one generation to the next. It also seemed strange that apprenticeships—the side-by-side training process whereby a youth acquired proficiency by inheriting both the skills and the experiences of an elder mentor—had been abandoned.

By way of contrast, the level of activity in corporate and business history in countries like the United States, Germany, and Japan was significantly higher, although the evidence there, too, was of an under exploited resource.

For the United Kingdom at least, the author's conclusion was that, without any corporate or business history to connect the generations, there was very little inheritance or continuity at both the wider industrial and individual organizational levels. In effect, each new generation of workers was obliged to virtually reinvent the wheel for themselves when they first entered the workforce and whenever they joined new companies. Yes, the lateral movement of employees across the workforce provided a constant source of new ideas for employers, but without access to their own employer's experience, this also meant that corporate requirements were increasingly being driven in isolation to their own experiences and circumstances.

At about the time the author's interest in OM was gestating, the importance of—and relationship between—hindsight and continuity then reinforced themselves in another event. The author was listening to a BBC radio program on heavyweight boxers in which one of the 1930s champions was explaining how he had beaten his opponent. One of the boxer's throwaway lines in the archive crackle was that he had spent time examining the newsreel footage of his opponent's previous fight and, from that, was able to derive a strategy to beat his adversary. It struck him that the film clip the boxer had seen all those years ago was, to all intents and purposes, the sporting equivalent of OM and that the individual was using experience—this time someone else's experience that wasn't distorted by time or ego—as a learning tool.

The author's imagination then took flight. Was not the boxer the forerunner of hundreds of thousands of other sportsmen and women who, since then, have accelerated their performances to an extent greater than in any previous period in history? Of course, training techniques had improved, as had athletes' diets, medical procedures, and that prime incentive, money, but—he asked himself—could their employment of "memory" in this way also be a factor in the dramatic improvement in performances over almost the entire range of sports? The fact that film and video usage in sports reporting has been around for about the same amount of time—and that most top sportsmen and women routinely use the medium to examine their own and each other's performances— seemed not uncoincidental. There had to be a relationship between historical awareness and decision making perspicacity. Thus began a quarter-century inquiry into how employers could *capture* and, importantly, *apply* their own prior knowledge and experience in a business environment where the memory of a job-for-life was as rare as the proverbial hen's tooth.

Then along came the discovery of the work of David Kolb and many of his predecessors and successors that refined the broader concept of how people best learned. This overlapped with the beginnings of the flexible labor market, which didn't at first register its true colors. Like most others—an observation that still survives to this day—it was interpreted as a long-overdue device to enable employers to adjust their staff requirements to rapidly-changing circumstances. Clearly, more flexibility in the labor market would also give employees broader experience that would make them more employable. All true, until the realization that all this movement didn't seem to be all that beneficial from the consumer's viewpoint. Inflation, poor service, and continual provider excuses all deafened the marketplace. Surely all that wider experience should prevent all this?

The other epiphany moment came when it was realized that companies and other types of organizations were rapid-fire trading their own experience for someone else's experience and that the replacement's experience was not necessarily relevant or even transferable in the time it took for employees to move on. In effect, employers were, quite unwittingly, allowing their most valuable asset—their experience, knowledge and wisdom—to walk out of the front door, leaving them with very little on which to build. Because all these institutions were unique, even within same industries or sectors, they were, in effect, having to re-invent themselves every generational change. Even perceived "star" replacements would have to be inducted into their new employers' culture and way of working. On the basis of their lower productivity for the first 12 months and reduced productivity in the last 12 months of their typical tenure of around four to five years, employers were not getting particularly good value from their employees.

Ironically, the beginnings of the flexible labor market wasn't too far removed from the days before side mirrors were installed on British cars. Then, one had to continually crane one's head to make navigational decisions. At best, drivers would get themselves a stiff neck; at worse, they would have a fatal accident. It was a time to install the business equivalent of more rear view mirrors.

Notes

Author's Credentials

1. Kransdorff (1998).
2. Kransdorff (2006b).

Chapter 1

1. G. Santayana, *The Life of Reason,* Prometheus Books (1998).
2. Groningen Growth and Development Centre and The Conference Board, Total Economy Database, August 2004.
3. An early sports example of modern experiential learning goes back to the 1930s when a heavyweight boxer was explaining on BBC Radio how he had beaten his opponent. One of his throwaway lines in the archive crackle was that he had spent time examining the newsreel footage of his opponent's previous fight and, from that, was able to derive a strategy to beat his adversary.
4. The word knowledge comes from the Saxon word *cnaw-lec.* The suffix *lec* has become, in modern English, *-like.* So, *knowledge* means "*cnaw*-like," with *cnaw* meaning "emerge". Its best interpretation, then, is that it is an emergent phenomenon, an extension of existing erudition.
5. Goldman (1999).
6. Aune (1967).
7. Allee (2002).
8. Wiig (2003).
9. Groysberg, Nanda, and Nohria (2004). In their investigation into poaching, which represents a large proportion of executive and vocational churn in the mercurial labour market, the researchers found that the performance of high flyers fell sharply and stayed well below old achievement levels thereafter. A total of 46% performed poorly in the year after they left one company for another. After they switched loyalties, their performance plummeted by an average of about 20% and did not climb back to the old levels even after five years.
10. Olivera (2000). This study finds that many managers only use their employer's archives sparingly, often complaining that source material is inadequate.
11. Polyany (1967). Polyany was the first to identify this category of knowledge in 1958.

12. de Bono (1977). The description of tacit knowledge given by Edward de Bono, the inventor of lateral thinking. He also called it the "skill of action."
13. The description of tacit knowledge given by Peter Drucker identified in the use of the word *techne* (Greek for "skill"). Drucker was an influential writer, management consultant, and self-described "social ecologist."
14. Yates (1990).
15. Nonaka and Tekeuchi (1995).
16. Labour Party Conference (1998); Mintel (2004).
17. Kantrow (1984).
18. Bonner (2000); Lee (2000); Smith (2001); Wah (1999).
19. Malthus and Ricardo's classical interpretation of The Law of Diminishing Returns attributes the successive diminishment of output to the decreasing quality of the inputs.
20. Groysberg et al. (2004).
21. Proudfoot Consulting (2005, September).
22. Carr (1972); J. L. Carr, "*I've never been spoken to like this before in all my thirty years' experience,*" she wails. "*You have not had thirty years' experience, Mrs Grindle-Jones,*" he says witheringly. "*You have had one year's experience 30 times.*"
23. Hayes (1984).
24. Kendrick (2009); O'Sullivan (2009).
25. Stability and Growth Pact (2011, March).

Chapter 2

1. Drucker (1991).
2. Byrne and Gerdes (2005).
3. Drucker (1991).
4. Groningen Growth and Development Centre and The Conference Board (2004).
5. There are a number of ways productivity is calculated, not all of them straightforward. For national productivity statistics, one formula is to take an estimate of aggregate output such as real gross domestic product (GDP)—the total unduplicated value of economic goods and services originating within the boundaries of a country—and divide it by the number of workers or the number of hours worked. These estimates are often described as "labor productivity," a computation muddied by issues such as national working hours, numbers in employment, and strike rates. Using this form of calculation, it is tempting to conclude that productivity is automatically enhanced if working hours are increased, more people are employed, or work stoppages reduced. Not necessarily. The British work the longest hours in Europe, yet its productivity is below—in fact substantially below—many of its competitors in

Europe and North America. A second formula uses a more comprehensive definition of inputs into the production process; the result is referred to as multifactor, or total-factor, productivity. The statistic is estimated by dividing the product of a broad sector by an input index that is a weighted average of two indexes, one of labor inputs and the other of capital inputs. The former—a quality-adjusted labor index—is a calculation of a weighted average of employee-hours for several groups of workers defined by sex, the level of education, and experience while the capital input index is a weighted average of capital services from many different categories of structures, equipment, inventories, and land. Many economists construct their own numbers. In the GDP-divided-by-population formula, employment, or employee-hours, are sometimes used instead of population. In calculating estimates of multifactor productivity, some analysts also distinguish between skilled and unskilled labor or between privately-owned and government-owned physical capital. At the industry level estimates are often constructed from figures representing value added rather than gross output. But productivity's most straightforward measure, at least at the individual company or organizational level, is probably the more simple calculation of dividing sales or operating budgets by employee headcount on a departmental, regional, or group basis. On its own, the number is meaningless. Where it becomes helpful is if the calculation is compared with prior data and, even more valuable, if it is measured against one's competitors. A lower comparison, for example, means that one's contenders are doing the same thing more effectively more cheaply. When a rival is more competitive, an organization's durability, even survival, is threatened.

6. Drucker (1991).
7. Groningen Growth and Development Centre and The Conference Board (2004).
8. Webb (1998).
9. Webb (1998).
10. Research, World Economic Forum (2002).
11. http://www.oecd.org/topicstatsportal/0,2647,en_2825_30453906_1_1_1_1_1,00.html
12. Groningen Growth and Development Centre and The Conference Board, Total Economy Database (2004).
13. Carlson and Rowe (1976).
14. Research, Corporate Leadership Council (1998).
15. Ledford and Lucy (2003).
16. KASE Consulting Group Ltd. and Integral Training Systems, Inc. (2003).
17. National Westminster Bank (1994).
18. Drucker (1981).
19. Dorgan and Dowdy (2002).

20. Kransdorff (2006).
21. Kantrow (1984).
22. Harvard Professor Chris Argyris is one of the main exponents of The Learning Organization's precepts (Argyris, 1991).
23. T. C. Barry, former President and Chief Executive Officer of New York-based Rockefeller & Co. and President of Marlboro, quoted in *Harvard Business Review*, July/August 1991.
24. Kransdorff (2006).
25. Drucker (1991).
26. Taylor (1911).
27. Gilbreth Jr. and Gilbreth (2003).
28. Mayo (1977).
29. *How to Build Quality* (1989).
30. Hutchins (1985).
31. McGregor (1960).
32. Drucker (1999).
33. Drucker (1973).
34. Haag, Cummings, McCubbrey, Pinsonneault, and Donovan (2006).
35. Thomas (2005).
36. Drucker (2003).

Chapter 3

1. Hoffer (1974).
2. Baumard (1999).
3. NZ Herald (2003).
4. Brown and Duguid (2000).
5. *Los Angeles Times* (1995).
6. *Personnel Today* (1977, July).
7. Kransdorff and Williams (1999).
8. Schön (1983).
9. Incremental knowledge is the product of prior experience that is already established and recognized—so-called "organic learning" that builds one experience on another (also known as *existent* or *historical knowledge*). It is the most common form of learning.
10. Accidental knowledge happens unexpectedly—such as what happened in 1928 when a mould spore drifted onto a culture dish in the laboratory of Scottish research scientist Alexander Fleming while he was on a two-week vacation. It seeded penicillin that killed off a harmful bacterium.
11. Innovative knowledge is the labor of genius, such as the work of Leonardo de Vinci who, in the late 15th century, conceptualized cutting-edge ideas like

the aeroplane, the parachute, cranes, submarines, tanks, water pumps, canals, and drills. Innovative knowledge encompasses the type of learning that leapfrogs the other types, and—in da Vinci's case—was so advanced that it had to wait hundreds of years for incremental learning to catch up.

12. Goffin and Koners (2011).
13. Lam (2000).
14. Kransdorff (1998).
15. Quoted in *What Colour is your parachute*, Bolles (1983).
16. BNA Inc., publisher of analysis, and reference products (2003).
17. OECD annual report (1992).
18. Employment Policy Institute, London (1997).
19. Labour Party Conference, Blackpool, U.K. (1998, September 28).
20. Research, Chartered Institute of Personnel and Development (CIPD) (2001).
21. Cantos (corporate research and broadcast company) survey (2003, June).
22. Employment Policy Institute, London (1997).
23. Mintel (2004).
24. Business Matters magazine (2012).
25. Kransdorff (2006).

Chapter 4

1. Groningen Growth and Development Centre and the Conference Board (2004).
2. Mintzberg and Lampel (2001).
3. Pfeffer & Fong (2002); Pfeffer is Professor of Organizational Behavior at the Stanford University business school. Fong is assistant professor of management and organization at the Foster School of Business who won a recent University of Washington Distinguished Teaching Award.
4. Hamel, Crainer, and Dearlove (1999).
5. Leavitt (1989).
6. Gaddis (2000).
7. Gaddis (2000).
8. Armstrong (1995).
9. Barron and Fisk (1985).
10. Pfeffer and Fong (2002).
11. Pfeffer and Fong (2002).
12. Driver (1999).
13. *Financial Times* (1997, March 5).
14. Porter (1996).
15. *Daily Telegraph* (1987, November 11).
16. *The Times* (1986, March 21).

17. *The Observer* (1985, October 6).
18. Council for Excellence in Management and Leadership (2002).
19. *Financial Times* (1998, April 29).
20. Norris (1997).
21. Leonhardt (2000).
22. Leonhardt (2000).
23. Lieber (1999).
24. Robinson (1994).
25. Godin (2000).
26. Davis and Botkin (1994).
27. *The Observer* (2002, January 13).
28. Management Education Task Force (2003).
29. Porter and McKibbin (1998).
30. Jenkins and Reizenstein (1984).
31. Mintzberg and Gosling (2002).
32. Advisory Panel on Management Education (1971).
33. Constable and McCormick (1987); Handy (1987).
34. Bailey and Ford (1996).
35. Leavitt (1989).
36. Brookfield (1990).
37. Mintzberg (2006, March 22).
38. Harte (2001).
39. *Business History Newsletter* (1984).
40. Fletcher (1988).
41. Author research.
42. Hunt and Downing (1991).
43. Correspondence with author (1992).
44. Interview with author.
45. Mintzberg and Lampel (2001).
46. Bailey and Ford (1996).
47. *Proudfoot Consulting* (2005, September).
48. The Centre for History of Chemistry (CHOC) (undated).
49. Capgemini (2004); Admission retrieved from http://www.businessschooladmission.com/teaching_methods.asp
50. *Daily Telegraph* (2004, October 23); Figures include £797 million by the Department for International Development, including research, £293 million by the Department for Transport, £2,623 million by Ministry of Defence, £10 million by the Department of Health, £15 million by the Cabinet Office, £52 million by the Office of the Deputy Prime Minister, £291 million by the Department for Work and Pensions and £10 million by the Scotland Office.
51. Capgemini (2004).

52. Rooke and Torbert (2005); Rooke is a consultant with Harthill Consulting and Torbert is a professor at the Carroll School of Management in Boston.
53. *Yahoo* (2005, April 6).
54. Hayes (1984).

Chapter 5

1. Bierce (1881–1906).
2. Hayes (1984).
3. Macintyre (2002).
4. Proudfoot Consulting (2005, September).
5. HM Treasury. Revenue relating to activities comprises mainly direct and indirect taxes, but also social security contributions, interest, dividends, capital taxes and profits from trading activities. Proceeds from the sale of assets are not included.
6. Cockerall (2010).
7. Analysis by the respected think tank, the Institute for Government (2012, February).
8. The Independent (2012, February 6).
9. The Independent (2012, April 2).
10. Daily Mail (2012, April 3).
11. National Audit Office study (2009, February).
12. National Audit Office Report (2008, September).
13. *The Times*, London (2003, April 26).
14. BAA report (1993).
15. Various press reports, including *We Cannot Pretend Lessons Were Learned*, Europe Intelligence Wire, March 22, 2006; *Food Safety Alters Europe's Farms*, Christian Science Monitor, March 20, 2001; *U.K. Economy, The Cost of Foot-and-Mouth*, Viewswire, July 29, 2002; and *U.K. Health News*, all daily summaries of health stories appearing in U.K. national newspapers for *British Medical Journal* online by Presswatch Media, at http://bmj.bmj journals.com/uknews/news20040108.shtml#6
16. Craig (2008).
17. *The Economist* (1996).
18. Utterbach (1994).
19. Abrahamson (2000).
20. Abrahamson (2000).
21. *The Economist* (1996, April 20).
22. *New Tools for Managing Workforce Stability and Engagement*, Washington-based Corporate Leadership Council (1998).
23. *New Tools for Managing Workforce Stability and Engagement*, Washington-based Corporate Leadership Council (1998).

24. *New Tools for Managing Workforce Stability and Engagement*, Washington-based Corporate Leadership Council (1998).
25. Lord Alexander, chairman of the National Westminster Bank.
26. de Geus (1988).
27. Occupational Safety and Health Administration press release (2009, October 30).
28. National Commission on the BP Deepwater Horizon Oil Spill and Offshore Drilling Report, July 2011.
29. *NY Times* (2010, July 12).
30. *NY Times* (2010, July 12).
31. U.S. Department of Labor, Bureau of Statistics, total non-farming separations (not seasonally adjusted), Job Openings and Labor Turnover survey.
32. *Fortune* (2006, October 31).
33. BP Report and Accounts (2008, December).
34. BP Report and Accounts (2012).
35. Bush (2009).
36. Blair (2003).
37. Malik (2003); Interview conducted by Peter Engardio and Thalif Deen. World Chronicle. New York: News & Media Division, Department of Public Information, United Nations.
38. The way multiple endowments over the years are grossed up to adjust for inflation is an inexact science, making the actual figure variable. Hollaway's quoted figure compares with an earlier estimate of nearly a trillion dollars since the 1960s to 2005. Richard Dowden, director of the Royal African Society, in an article to coincide with the BBC2 TV program *If… We Stop Giving Aid to Africa*, June 26, 2005, admitted then that "*much of Africa is worse off now than it was then.*" The comparison with the multiple of Marshall Plans seems more consistent—about five, according to Ian Vásquez, director of the Project on Global Economic Liberty at the Cato Institute, in an article in the Washington Times, July 8, 2005.
39. Zenawi (2000); Remarks in speech at Harvard University, recorded in Policy Research Working Paper 248. New York: The World Bank Development Research Group.
40. Groningen Growth and Development Centre and The Conference Board, 2004.

Chapter 6

1. Hoffer (1974).
2. Terkel (1984).
3. Everett (1992).

4. Kraske, Becker, Diamond, and Galambos (1997).
5. Reader (1975).
6. Interview with author.

Chapter 7

1. Hoban (1973).
2. Ivan Petrovich Pavlov was the Nobel prize-winning Russian physiologist who developed the concept of Classical Conditioning, a form of learning in which one stimulus signals the occurrence of a second stimulus. His classic experiment was to present dogs with a ringing bell followed by food, which elicited salivation. Repeated events led to salivation after bell ringing.
3. Piaget (1951).
4. *Time Magazine* (1999, March 29).
5. Dewey (1916).
6. Freire (1985).
7. Lewin (1951).
8. Bloom (1965).
9. Maslow (1937).
10. Gagne (1987).
11. Argyris and Schön (1974).
12. Saljo (1982).
13. Mezirow (2000).
14. Gregorc (1998).
15. Rogers (1969).
16. Wenger (1999).
17. Perls (1973).
18. Mayo (1949).
19. Senge (1990).
20. Revans (1980).
21. Schön (1993).
22. Kegan (1982).
23. Klein (2007).
24. Goleman (2005).
25. Reynolds and Vince (Eds.) (2007).
26. Reynolds and Vince (Eds.) (2007).
27. Dehler (2006).
28. Lewis, Welsh, and Dehler (2002).
29. Torbert (1991).
30. Le Heron and Sligo (2005).
31. Nonaka (1995).
32. Kolb (1984).

Chapter 8

1. C. Darwin, *On the Origin of Species by Means of Natural Selection*, various publishers.
2. Drucker (1999).
3. *Chicago Tribune* (1916); Henry Ford's affirmation of experience's lack of authority took 8 days of cross-examination in a successful court case for libel against the *Chicago Tribune*, which had described him as an "anarchist" and "ignorant idealist."

Appendix

1. Hannah (1981).

References

Abrahamson, E. (2000, July–August). Change without pain. *Harvard Business Review.*

Advisory Panel on Management Education. (1971). *The requirements of British manufacturing industry: Business school programmes.* London: British Institute of Management and Council of Industry for Management Education.

Allee, V. (2002). *The future of knowledge: Increasing prosperity through value networks.* Boston, MA: Butterworth-Heinemann.

Analysis by the respected think tank, the Institute for Government (2012, February).

Approaches to psychology. (1999, March 29). *Time Magazine.*

Argyris, C. (1991, May/June). Teaching smart people how to learn. *Harvard Business Review.*

Argyris, C., & Schön, D. A. (1974). *Theory in practice: Increasing professional effectiveness.* Oxford, UK: Jossey-Bass.

Armstrong, S. (1995). The devil's advocate responds to an MBA student's claim that research harms learning. *Journal of Marketing.*

Aune, B. (1967). *Knowledge, mind, and nature: An introduction to theory of knowledge and the philosophy of mind.* New York, NY: Random House.

Bailey, J., & Ford, C. (1996). Management as science versus management as practice in postgraduate business education. *Business Strategy Review.*

Barron, R. & Fisk, J. (1985). *Great Business Quotations.*

Baumard, P. (1999). *Tacit knowledge in organizations.* London, UK: Sage Publications.

Bierce, A. (1881–1906). *The Devil's Dictionary.*

Blair, T. (2003, January 20). Speech to the U.S. Congress. Washington, press release.

Bloom, B. (1965). *Stability and change in human characteristics.* New York, NY: Wiley.

Bolles, R. (1983). *What color is your parachute?* Berkeley, CA: Ten Speed Press.

Bonner, D. (2000), *Knowledge: From theory to practice to golden opportunity.* American Society for Training & Development.

de Bono, E. (1977). *The use of lateral thinking.* London, UK: Cape.

Brookfield, S. (1990). *The skilful teacher.* San Francisco: Jossey-Bass.

Brown, J., & Duguid, P. (2000). *The social life of information.* Boston, MA: Harvard Business School Press.

Bush, G. (2009, January 12). Final press conference.

Business Matters. (2012, April 12). *Social networking creates a nation of job flirts.* U.K. social talent management report.

Byrne, J. A., & Gerdes, L. (2005, November 28). The man who invented management. *Business Week*.

Capgemini. (2004, August). *U.K. Business Decisiveness Report*. Capgemini.

Carlson, J. G., & Rowe, A. J. (1976). How much does forgetting cost? *Industrial Engineering 8*(9), 40–47.

Carr, J. L. (1972). *Harpole report*. London, UK: Secker and Warburg.

Cockerall, M. (screened February 18, 2010). *The Great Offices of State*, BBC.

Constable, J., & McCormick, R. (1987, April). *The making of British managers: A Report for the BIM and CBI into management training, education and development*. Corby: British Institute of Management.

Craig, D. (2008). *Squandered*. London, UK: Constable & Robinson.

Darwin, C. *On the Origin of Species by Means of Natural Selection*, various publishers.

Davenport, T. H. (2005). *Thinking for a living*. Boston, MA: Harvard Business Review Press.

Davis, S., & Botkin, J. (1994). *The monster under the bed: How business is mastering the opportunity of knowledge for profit*. New York, NY: Simon and Schuster.

Dehler, G. (2006). Using action research to connect practice to learning: A course project for working management students. *Journal of Management Education 20*(2), 221–235.

Dewey, J. (1916). *Democracy and education: An introduction to the philosophy of education*. New York, NY: Free Press.

Dorgan, S. J., & Dowdy, J. J. (2002). How good management raises productivity. *The McKinsey Quarterly 4*, 14–16.

Driver, C. (1999). *Investment, growth, and employment: Perspectives for policy*. London, UK: Routledge.

Drucker, P. F. (1973). *Management: Tasks, responsibilities, practices*. New York, NY: Harper & Row.

Drucker, P. F. (1981). *Managing in turbulent times*. London, UK: Macmillan.

Drucker, P. F. (1991, Nov/Dec). The new productivity challenge. *Harvard Business Review 69*(6).

Drucker, P. F. (1999). *Management challenges for the 21st century*. Butterworth-Heinemann.

Drucker, P. F. (2003). *Peter Drucker on the profession of management*. Boston, MA: Harvard Business Press.

The Economist. (1989, September 23). *How to Build Quality*, 91–92.

The Economist. (1996, April 20). *Fire and forget*.

Everett, S. E. (1992). *Oral history techniques and procedures*. Washington, DC: Center of Military History, United States Army.

Fletcher, A. (1988). *Speech*.

Fortune. (2006, October 31). *Can BP bounce back?*

Freire, P. (1985). *The politics of education*. Westport, CT: Greenwood.

Gaddis, P. O. (2000). Business schools: Fighting the enemy within. *Strategy and Business*.

Gagne, R. (1987). *Instructional technology: Foundations*. Philadelphia: Lawrence Erlbaum Associates.

de Geus, A. (1988, March–April). Planning as learning. *Harvard Business Review*.

Gilbreth Jr., F. B., & Gilbreth, E. (2003). *Cheaper by the dozen*. Cary, Carey (Mass Market Paperback).

Godin, S. (2000, September).*Change agent*. Fast Company.

Goffin, K., & Koners, U. (2011). Tacit knowledge, lessons learnt, and new product development. *Journal of Product Innovation Management 28*, 300–318.

Goldman, A. (1999). *Knowledge in a social world*. Oxford, UK: Clarendon Press.

Goleman, D. (2005). *Emotional intelligence*. Bantam Books.

Gregorc, A. (1998). *The mind style model*. Connecticut: Gregorc Associates.

Groningen Growth and Development Centre and The Conference Board, Total Economy Database. (2004, August). Available at: http://www.ggdc.net

Groysberg, B., Nanda, A., & Nohria, N. (2004, May). The risky business of hiring stars. *Harvard Business Review*.

Haag, S., Cummings, M., McCubbrey, D., Pinsonneault, A., & Donovan, R. (2006). *Management information systems for the information age* (3rd Canadian ed.), Canada: McGraw Hill Ryerson.

Hamel, G., Crainer, S., & Dearlove, D. (1999). *Gravy training: Inside the business of business schools*. San Francisco, CA: Jossey-Bass.

Handy, C. (1987). *The making of managers: A report on management education, training and development in the USA, West Germany, France, Japan and the U.K.* London, UK: National Economic Development Office.

Hannah, L. (1981). *New horizons for business history*. London, UK: Social Science Research Council.

Harte, N. (2001). Economic History Society.

Hayes, R. (1984). *The timeless secrets of industrial success* (Classroom discussion paper). Harvard Business School.

Hoban, R. (1973). *The Lion of Boaz-Jachin and Jachin-Boaz*. Cape.

Hoffer, E. (1974). *Reflections on the human condition*. Reader's Digest (Australia) Pty Ltd.

Hunt, J., & Downing, S. (1991). *The human factor*. London Business School Research.

Hutchins, D. C. (1985). *The quality circles handbook*. New York, NY: Pitman Press.

The Independent. (2012, February 6). *Turnover of top staff risks leaving civil service short of expertise*.

The Independent. (2012, April 2). *Margaret Hodge: The granny with Sir Humphrey in her crosshairs.*

Jenkins, R. L., & Reizenstein, R. C. (1984). Insights into the MBA: Its contents, output, and relevance. *Selections: The Magazine of the Graduate Management Admission Council 1*(1), 19–24.

Kantrow, A. M. (1984). *The constraints of corporate tradition.* New York, NY: Harper & Row.

KASE Consulting Group Ltd. and Integral Training Systems, Inc. (2003). *Study into staff turnover costs.*

Kegan, R. (1982). *Evolving self.* Cambridge, MA: Harvard University Press.

Kendrick, J. W. (1952). *Productivity trends in the United States.* Princeton, NJ: Princeton University Press.

Klein, S. (2007). *Biological psychology.* New York, NY: Worth Publishers.

Kolb, D. (1984). *Experiential learning: Experience as a source of learning and development.* London, UK: Financial Times/Prentice-Hall.

Kransdorff, A. (1998). *Corporate amnesia.* London, UK: Butterworth Heinemann.

Kransdorff, A., & Williams, R. (1999). Swing doors and musical chairs. *Business Horizons 42*(3), 27–32.

Kransdorff, A. (2006). *Begging for a bigger role.* New York, NY: Business Expert Press.

Kransdorff, A. (2006). *Corporate DNA.* London, UK: Gower.

Kraske, J., Becker, W. H., Diamond, W., & Galambos, L. (1997). *Bankers with a mission.* New York, NY: OUP USA/World Bank.

Lam, A. (2000). *Knowledge, organizational learning and societal institutions: An integrated framework.* Canterbury, UK: Canterbury Business School, University of Kent.

Leavitt, H. J. (1989). Educating our MBAs: On teaching what we haven't taught. *California Management Review 31*(3), 38.

Ledford, G., & Lucy, M. (2003). *The rewards of work: The employment deal in a changing economy.* New York, NY: Sibson Consulting, The Segal Group.

Le Heron, J., & Sligo, F. (2005). *Acquisition of simple and complex knowledge: A knowledge gap perspective.* Educational Technology & Society.

Leonhardt, D. (2000, October 1). A matter of degree? Not for consultant. *New York Times.*

Lewin, K. (1951). *Field theory in social sciences.* New York, NY: Harper & Row.

Lewis, M., Welsh, M., & Dehler, G. (2002). *Product development tensions: Exploring contrasting styles of project management.* Academy of Management Journals.

Lieber, R. (1999, December). *Learning and change: Roger Martin.* Fast Company.

Macintyre, B. (2002). *The Times.* London.

Malik, K. (2003, November 13). Interview conducted by Peter Engardio and Thalif Deen. *World Chronicle*. New York, NY: News & Media Division, Department of Public Information, United Nations.

Management Education Task Force, Association to Advance. (2003). *Management education at risk*. Tampla, FL: Collegiate Schools of Business.

Maslow, A. (1937). *Psychology of personality*. Boston, MA: McGraw-Hill.

Mayo, E. (1977). *The human problems of an industrialized civilization*. Salem, NY: Ayer Co.

Mayo, G. E. (1949). *The social problems of an industrial civilisation*. International Library of Sociology. London, UK: Routledge and Kegan Paul.

McGregor, D. (1960). *The human side of enterprise*. New York, NY: McGraw Hill.

Mezirow, J. (2000). *Learning as transformation: Critical perspectives on a theory in progress*. John Wiley & Sons.

Mintel (2004 , November). *British lifestyles*.

Mintzberg, H., & Gosling, J. R. (2002). Reality programming for MBAs. *Strategy and Business*.

Mintzberg, H., & Lampel, J. (2001, February 19). Matter of degrees: Do MBAs make better CEOs? *Fortune*.

Mintzberg, H. (2006). The nature of managerial work. *International Journal of Commerce and Management*.

National Westminster Bank (1994). *Review of small business trends*. London: Small Business Research Trust.

New York Times. (2010, July 12). *In BP's record, a history of boldness and costly blunders*.

Nonaka, I. (1995). *The knowledge-creating company: How Japanese companies create the dynamics of innovation*. Oxford, UK: Oxford University Press.

Nonaka, I., & Tekeuchi, H. (1995). *The knowledge-creating company*. New York, NY: Oxford University Press.

Norris, F. H. (1997, January 2). The crimson crop is plenty green. *New York Times*.

Olivera, F. (2000, September). Memory systems in organizations: An empirical investigation of mechanisms for knowledge collection, storage and access. *Journal of Management Studies 37*, 811–832.

O'Sullivan, A. (2009). *Urban economics* (7th ed.). New York, NY: McGraw-Hill Higher Education.

Perls, F. (1973). *The gestalt approach and eyewitness to therapy*. Pala Alto, CA: Science and Behavior Books.

Pfeffer, J., & Fong, C. (2002, September). The end of business schools? Less success than meets the eye. *Academy of Management Learning & Education 1*(1).

Piaget, J. (1951). *Play, dreams and imitation in childhood*. W.W. Norton.

Polyany, M. (1967). *The tacit dimension*. Garden City, NY: Anchor Books.

Porter, L. W., & McKibbin, L. E. (1998). *Management education and development: Drift or thrust into the 21st century.* New York, NY: McGraw-Hill.

Porter, M. (1996, March). Institute of Personnel Development annual training conference.

Proudfoot Consulting. (2005, September).

Reader, B. (1975). *In dictatorship in the '30s, Barons revolt.* ICI history.

Revans, R. (1980). *Action learning.* Frederick Muller.

Reynolds, M., & Vince, R. (Eds.) (2007). *Handbook on experiential learning.* Oxford, UK: Oxford University Press.

Robert, H. (1984). *The timeless secrets of industrial success* (classroom discussion paper). Harvard Business School.

Robinson, P. (1994). *Snapshots from Hell.* New York, NY: Warner Books.

Rogers, C. (1969). *Freedom to learn.* Columbus, OH: Merrill.

Rooke, D., & Torbert, W. (2005, April). *Transformations of leadership.* Harvard Business Review.

Saljo, R. (1982). *Learning and understanding.* New York, NY: Springer.

Santayana, G. (1998). *The life of reason.* Amherst, NY: Prometheus Books.

Schön, D. (1983). *Reflective practitioner: How professionals think in action.* London, UK: Maurice Temple Smith.

Schön, D. A. (1993). *The reflective practitioner.* New York, NY: Basic Books.

Senge, P. (1990). *The fifth discipline: The age and practice of The Learning Organization.* London, UK: Century Business.

Smith, E. A. (2001). The role of tacit and explicit knowledge in the workplace. *Journal of Knowledge Management 5*(4), 311–321.

Stability and Growth Pact (2012, April 27). Statement by José Manuel Barroso and Mario Monti that "growth must come through a relentless focus on improving competitiveness…". http://www.europolitics.info/economy-monetary-affairs/growth-but-how-art332944-50.html

Taylor, W. F. (1911). *Principles of scientific management.* New York and London: Harper & Brothers.

Terkel, S. (1984). *Envelopes of sound: The art of oral history.* Chicago: Precedent.

Torbert, W. (1991). *The power of balance.* Newbury Park, CA: Sage.

Utterbach, J. (1994). *Mastering the dynamics of innovation.* Harvard Business School Press.

Wah, L. (1999). Making knowledge stick. *Management Review*, May, pp. 24–29.

Washington-Based Corporate Leadership Council. (1998). *New tools for managing workforce stability and engagement.*

Webb, R. H. (1998). National productivity statistics. *U.K. Federal Reserve Bank of Richmond Economic Quarterly 84*(1), 45–64.

Wenger, E. (1999). *Communities of practice: Learning, meaning, and identity.* Cambridge University Press.

Wiig, K. (2003). *A knowledge model for situation-handling.* Arlington, TX: Knowledge Research Institute, Inc.

Yates, J. (1990). *For the record: Embodiment of organizational memory, 1859–1920,* Business and economic history, Second Series, Volume 19.

Zenawi, M., (2000, September 5). *Remarks in speech at Harvard University* (recorded in Policy Research Working Paper 248). New York, NY: The World Bank Development Research Group.

Bibliography

Abernathy, W., & Corcoran, J. (1983, August). Relearning from the old masters. *Journal of Operations Management.*

Anderlohr, G. (1969). Determining the cost of production breaks. *Management Review 58*(12).

Argyris, C., & Schön, D. A. (1978). *Organizational learning.* Addison-Wesley.

Argyris, C. (1997, September/October). Double loop learning in organizations. *Harvard Business Review.*

Bailey, C. D., & McIntyre, E. V. V. (1992, April). Some evidence on the nature of relearning curves. *Accounting Review.*

Bateson, G. (1979). *Mind and nature: A necessary unity.* New York: Bantam Books.

Bateson, G. (1973). *Steps to an ecology of mind.* London: Paladin.

Boulding, K. E. (1956). *The image: Knowledge in life and society.* Ann Arbor: University of Michigan.

Bowen, H. K., Clark, K., Holloway, C., & Wheelwright, S. (1994). *The perpetual enterprise machine.* Oxford: Oxford University Press.

Bowker, G. C. (1997). Lest we remember: Organizational forgetting and the production of knowledge. *Accounting, Management, & Information Technology 7*(3).

Chandler, A. D. (1962). *Strategy and structure.* Cambridge, MA: MIT Press.

Clemens, J. (1978). *The classic touch: Lessons in leadership from Homer to Hemingway.* Dow Jones-Irwin.

de Geus, A. (1997). *The living company.* Boston: Harvard Business School Press.

Drucker, P. F. (1962). *Post-capitalist society.* Oxford: Butterworth Heinemann.

Drucker, P. F. (1989). *The new realities.* New York: Harper & Row.

Frisch, M. (1990). *Shared authority: Essays on the craft and meaning of oral and public history.* London: British Archives Council.

Garratt, B. (1989). *The Learning Organization.* Fontana.

Garratt, B. (1996). *The fish rots from the head.* Glasgow: HarperCollins.

Grele, R. J. (1991). *Envelopes of sound: The art of oral history.* London: British Archives Council.

Hamel, G., & Prahalad, C. K. (1994). *Competing for the future.* Boston, MA: Harvard Business School Press.

Herriot, P., & Pemberton, C. (1993). *Competitive advantage through diversity.* London: Sage.

Honey, P. (1991, July). The Learning Organization simplified. *Training & Development.*

Hurst, D. K. (1996). *Crisis and renewal: Meeting the challenge of organization change*. Boston: Harvard Business School Press.

Jones, G. (1994/1995). Business history: Theory and concepts. Discussion paper in economics, Series A, Vol. V11. Reading: University of Reading Department of Economics.

Kimberly, J. R., & Miles, R. H. (1980). *The organizational life cycle*. San Francisco: Jossey-Bass.

Kofman, F., & Senge, P. M. (1993). The heart of learning organizations. *Organization Dynamics 22*(2).

Leucke, R. A. (1994). *Scuttle your ships before advancing: And other lessons from history on leadership and change for today's managers*. Oxford: Oxford University Press.

Maidique, M. A., & Zirger, B. J. The new product learning cycle. *Research Policy, 14*(6).

Maira, A., & Scott-Morgan, P. (1997). *The accelerating organization*. McGraw-Hill.

Mbaye, S. (1988). *Oral archives*. London: ICA.

McCall, M. (1997). *High flyers: Developing the next generation of leaders*. Boston: Harvard Business School Press.

McCall, M., Lombardo, M., & Morrison, A. (1988). *The lessons of experience*. Lexington, MA: Lexington Books.

McClelland, C. A. (1958). *Systems history in international relations*. Louisville, KY: General Systems Yearbook.

Moss, W., & Mazikana, P. C. (1986). *Archives, oral history, and oral tradition*. RAMP.

Mumford, A. (1994). Four approaches to learning from experience. *The Learning Organization 1*(1).

Mumford, A., Honey, P., & Robinson, G. (1989). *Directors' development guidebook: Making experience count*. London: Training Agency/Institute of Directors.

Neustadt, R., & May, E. (1986). Thinking in time: The uses of history for decision maker.

Noer, D. (1993). *Healing the wounds: Overcoming the trauma of layoffs and revitalizing downsized organizations*. Jossey-Bass.

Nonaka, I., & Takeuchi, H. (1995). *The knowledge creating company*. New York: Oxford University Press.

Parsons, T., & Shils, E. A. (1962). *Towards a general theory of action*. New York: Harper & Row/Torchbooks.

Pedler, M., Burgoyne, J., & Boydell, T. (1991). *The learning company: A strategy for sustainable growth*. Maidenhead, U.K.: McGraw-Hill.

Peters, T. J., & Waterman, R. H. (1994). *In search of excellence*. London: Harper & Row.

Pfeffer, J. (1981). *Management as symbolic action in research in organizational behavior*. Greenwich, CT: JAI Press.

Polanyi, M. (1966). *The tacit dimension*. London: Routledge & Kegan Paul.

Quinn, J. B. (1992). *Intelligent enterprise: A knowledge and service-based paradigm for industry*. New York: Free Press.

Ritchie, D. A. (1995). *Doing oral history*. New York: Twayne Publishers.

Schein, E. H. (1985). *Organizational culture and leadership*. San Francisco: Jossey-Bass.

Smith, G. D., & Stedman, L. E. (1981, November/December). *The present value of corporate history*. Boston: Harvard Business Review.

Stewart, T. A. (1997). *Intellectual capital: The new wealth of organizations*. London: Nicholas Brealey.

Swieringa, J., & Wierdsma, A. (1992). *Becoming a learning organization: Beyond the learning curve*. Reading, MA: Addison-Wesley.

Terkel, S. (1995). *Good war oral history of WW2*. Ballantine.

Terkel, S. (1995). *Coming of age: The story of our century by those who've lived it*. Penguin.

Terkel, S. (1981). *American dream lost and found*. London: Hodder & Stoughton.

Terkel, S. (1984). *Envelopes of sound: The art of oral history*. Precedent Publications.

Terkel, S. (1988). *Hard times: An oral history of the Great Depression*. UK: Randon House.

Thompson, P. (1978). *The voice of the past: Oral history*. Oxford: Oxford University Press.

Tichy, N. M., with Cohen E. (1997). *The leadership engine*. New York: Harper Business.

Tofler, A. (1970). *Future shock*. New York: Bantam Books.

Tofler, A. (1990). *Powershift knowledge, wealth, and violence at the edge of the 21st century*. New York: Bantam Books.

Townsend, P. L., & Gebhardt, J. E. (1997). *Five-star leadership*. New York: John Wiley & Sons.

Walsh, J. P., & Ungson, G. R. (1990). *Organizational memory: Structure, functions and application*. Hanover, NH: Amos Tuck School of Business Administration.

Walsh, J. P. (1995). Managerial and organizational cognition: Notes from a trip down memory lane. *Organization Science 6*(3).

What Production Breaks Cost, Industrial Engineering, September 1969.

Index

A
Acquired wisdom, 2
Action-driven approaches, 100
After-action reviews, 88
Aid industry, 74
Annual average turnover rate, 36
Archival material, 84

B
Bankruptcy, 13
Barings crisis, 72
Behaviorialism, 97
Benchmarking, 84
Best alternatives, 52
Big Mac index, 18
Biographical debriefing, 85
Bovine spongiform encephalopathy
    (BSE), 64
BRICK countries, 18
Budget, 83
Bull-market times, 13
Business critical decisions, 53
Business-speeding technological
    advances, 21

C
Captive markets, 19
Capture-the-evidence stage, 80, 84
Chris Argyris–Donald Schön
    collaboration, 99
Chronic dependency culture, 75
Client funding, 46
Cliometrics, 46
Cognitive knowledge, 4
Collaborative decision making
    approach, 53
Competitiveness, 13
Constant staff turnover, 69
Conventional business instruction, 5
Coping skills, 4
Corporate amnesia, 2, 6, 8, 10, 19,
    21, 22, 35, 64, 84, 103–105

Corporate history, 46, 49, 90
Cost–benefit analysis, 52
Credit
    crisis, 74
    crunch, 70
Critical incident debriefing, 86
Cutbacks, 13
Cyclic models, 19

D
Day in, day out, 63
Decision making skew, 93
Decision-making tool, 30
Decision tree, 52, 93
Decision-making skills, 12
Decision-making styles, 53
Design memory, 64
Development projects, 82
Dialogue, 98
Discounting, 52
Documentation, 33, 89
Dot-com collapse, 71
Double-loop or reframing
    learning, 99
Downward drift, 18
Drucker's productivity challenge, 19

E
Eastern empiricism reasons, 4
EBM learning loop, 96
EBM's knowledge chart, 81
Economic
    crisis, 10
    history, 49
Edinburgh review, 57
Einstein-applauded observations, 57
Elteto-Köves-Szul method, 18
Employee
    numbers, 13
    transit audit, 83
Employer's knowledge, 2
EU economy, 17

Evaluation Stage, 80, 95
Evaluation, 95
Evolution, 23
Exit
  debriefing, 86
  interview, 86
Experience-based management
  (EBM), 79, 102
  capture-the-evidence
    stage, 80, 84
  evaluation stage, 80, 95
  lessons audit, 80, 93
  planning stage, 80, 81
  reflection module, 80, 92
  reprocessing stage, 80, 94
Experiential learning, 1, 5, 51, 67, 70,
  71, 73, 77, 92, 99
Experiential non-learning, 66, 69,
  70, 74
Explicit knowledge, 7, 30

F
Figurative word picture, 94
Finance sector, 66
Financial crisis, 73, 77
Financial deregulation, 71
Flexible market, 34
Forgetting phenomena, 19
Formal business education, 5
Freehold policies, 74, 76
Functional managers, 55

G
Global slump, 14
Good decision making, 33
Good judgement, 2
Groningen dataset, 18
Groningen's productivity databases, 18
Group thinking processes, 100

H
Human relations, 25

I
Imported experiences, 3
Incremental or single-loop learning, 99
Information society, 11
Information technology (IT)
  professionals, 30

Institutional memory loss, 21
Institution-specific experience, 7
Intellectual property, 30
International masters in practising
  management (IMPM), 45
Investment economy, 75

K
Knowledge
  capture device, 87
  capture process, 83
  chart, 81
  collection process, 77
  leaks, 83
  management (KM), 29, 34
  mapping, 81, 84
  retrieval plan, 83, 84
  storage technologies, 81
  workers, 26
Kolb's model of experiential learning,
  79, 101
Korean war effort, 73

L
Laissez-Faire capitalism, 73
Learning audit, 95
Learning cycle model, 20
Learning histories, 32, 68, 69
Learning life cycle, 19
Learning organization, 67, 100
Leasehold, 74, 75, 76
Leg-up, 93
Lender of last resort, 72
Lessons audit, 80, 93
Life cycle, 19
Long-term capital management
  (LTCM), 71

M
Management dysfunction, 58, 77
Management, 13
Managerial skills, 53
McKinsey Global Institute
  (MGI), 22
Multiple-loop learning, 100

N
New knowledge, 33
Non-technical how, 4

O

Occupational positions, 81
Occupational safety and health
    administration (OSHA), 67
OECD's productivity growth, 12
OECD's Structural Analysis
    database, 18
Open public services, 60
Operational-type suppositions, 93
Oral debriefing techniques, 32, 84,
    86, 87
Ordered evolution, 37
Organisation for Economic
    Cooperation and Development
    (OECD), 1, 8, 12, 14, 17, 58
Organization Memory (OM), 7,
    29, 37, 62, 65, 80, 84, 90, 93,
    95, 102
Organization-specific knowledge, 83
Ownership matters, 75, 76

P

Pavlovian view, 97, 98
Payback period, 52
Pilot projects, 76
Planning stage, 80, 81
Policy-making skills, 12
Present value, 52
Private land ownership, 74, 75
Productivity growth, 12, 13
Productivity measure, 12
Progress, 21
Project auditing, 82
Project map, 81, 84
Public accounts committee
    (PAC), 61, 62
Public ownership of private
    assets, 71
Purchasing power parity (PPP), 18

R

Reflection module, 80, 92
Reinventing wheels, 64
Reprocessing stage, 80, 94

S

School of hard knocks, 21
Self-protective policy, 74
Service workers, 27
Shell scandal, 67
Short jobs tenure, 10
Short-tenure employees, 8
Short-term experience, 4
Short-term memory, 7
Skilled interviewer, 86
Skilled knowledge, 4
Strategy-type conclusions, 93
Subject debriefing, 85
Subsistence plots, 76

T

Techne, 4
Too big to fail, 73
Total quality management
    (TQM), 25
Traditional knowledge mapping, 81
Transcripts, 32
Transformative learning, 100
Triple-loop learning, 100

V

Variant Creutzfeldt-Jakob disease
    (vCJD), 64
Vocational competence, 44

W

Washington-based corporate
    leadership council, 20
Wealth, 13
Western rationalism, 4
Wider trend, 18
Work smarter, 25
Workers, 21
Workforce, 6
Workplace practice, 2
Worldwide domino effects, 70

X

Xenophobia, 76

Announcing the Business Expert Press Digital Library

Concise E-books Business Students Need for Classroom and Research

This book can also be purchased in an e-book collection by your library as

- a one-time purchase,
- that is owned forever,
- allows for simultaneous readers,
- has no restrictions on printing, and
- can be downloaded as PDFs from within the library community.

Our digital library collections are a great solution to beat the rising cost of textbooks. e-books can be loaded into their course management systems or onto student's e-book readers.

The **Business Expert Press** digital libraries are very affordable, with no obligation to buy in future years. For more information, please visit **www.businessexpertpress.com/librarians**. To set up a trial in the United States, please contact **Adam Chesler** at *adam.chesler@businessexpertpress .com* for all other regions, contact **Nicole Lee** at *nicole.lee@igroupnet.com*.

OTHER TITLES IN OUR STRATEGIC MANAGEMENT COLLECTION

Collection Editor: **William Q. Judge**

- *Managing for Ethical-Organizational Integrity: Principles and Processes for Promoting Good, Right, and Virtuous Conduct* by Abe Zakhem
- *Corporate Bankruptcy: Fundamental Principles and Processes* by William J. Donoher
- *Moral Leadership: A Transformative Model for Tomorrow's Leaders* by Cam Caldwell
- *Learning Organizations: Turning Knowledge into Action* by Marcus Goncalves

www.ingramcontent.com/pod-product-compliance
Lightning Source LLC
Chambersburg PA
CBHW071848200326
41519CB00016B/4293